Download Forms

You can download the forms in this book at:

 www.nolo.com/back-of-book/PART.html

We'll also post updates whenever there's an important change to the law affecting this book—as well as articles and other related materials.

More Resources
from Nolo.com

Legal Forms, Books, & Software
Hundreds of do-it-yourself products—all written in plain English, approved, and updated by our in-house legal editors.

Legal Articles
Get informed with thousands of free articles on everyday legal topics. Our articles are accurate, up to date, and reader friendly.

Find a Lawyer
Want to talk to a lawyer? Use Nolo to find a lawyer who can help you with your case.

NOLO
LAW for ALL

11th Edition

Form a Partnership

The Legal Guide for Business Owners

Attorney Denis Clifford

ELEVENTH EDITION	AUGUST 2020
Editor	DIANA FITZPATRICK
Cover Design	SUSAN PUTNEY
Production	SUSAN PUTNEY
Proofreader	ROBERT WELLS
Index	ACCESS POINTS INDEXING
Printing	BANG PRINTING

Names: Clifford, Denis, author.
Title: Form a partnership : the complete legal guide / Attorney Denis
  Clifford.
Description: 11th edition. | Berkeley : Nolo, 2020. | Includes index.
Identifiers: LCCN 2020007199 (print) | LCCN 2020007200 (ebook) | ISBN
  9781413327892 (paperback) | ISBN 9781413327908 (ebook)
Subjects: LCSH: Partnership--United States--Popular works. | Articles of
  partnership--United States--Popular works.
Classification: LCC KF1375.Z9 C55 2020 (print) | LCC KF1375.Z9 (ebook) |
  DDC 346.73/0682--dc23
LC record available at https://lccn.loc.gov/2020007199
LC ebook record available at https://lccn.loc.gov/2020007200

This book covers only United States law, unless it specifically states otherwise.

Please note

We know that accurate, plain-English legal information can help you solve many of your own legal problems. But this text is not a substitute for personalized advice from a knowledgeable lawyer. If you want the help of a trained professional —and we'll always point out situations in which we think that's a good idea— consult an attorney licensed to practice in your state.

Acknowledgments

Putting together this edition of *Form a Partnership* was a major job. Without the editing help of many people, we would have produced a less thorough and less readable book, and had much less fun preparing it. So our gratitude and thanks to the following friends:

First, to our current editor, Diana Fitzpatrick, for her thorough editing of this edition, and to Tony Mancuso, Nolo's reigning guru on limited liability companies.

Second, we want to express our deep appreciation to all those who've helped in many editions of this book, all our previous editors, and Terri Hearsh, who laid out the manuscript with professional skill and a keen editor's eye. Next, to Kit Duane, an excellent editor, superb writer, and great friend. Moving on, several lawyer friends and partnership experts who graciously gave us considerable time to discuss what they (and we) have learned about partnerships: Lawrence A. Baskin, San Rafael, California; and Dick Duane (retired attorney). And several business friends who also greatly aided us in updating our understanding of partnerships: Ray Castor, Carla Jupiter, Steve Clifford, and Carol Kizziah. Also of great help have been the many thoughtful readers who've written us of their experiences forming partnerships. We've used many of these readers' suggestions to expand and deepen our coverage of partnership concerns in this edition.

Next, we want to thank the wonderful gang at Nolo. Collectively, they make it possible for us to bring you this book. In addition, we want to specifically thank a few Noloids who personally assisted with the editing and preparation of previous editions of the manuscript: Marcia Stewart, Stephanie Harolde, Barbara Hodovan, and Ann Heron.

Finally, we want to express our continued appreciation to others who helped us on previous editions: Hayden Curry, Marvin Cherrin, Tom Fike, Steve Antler, Bill Petrocelli, Marilyn Putnam, Brad Bunin, Patti Unterman, Chris Cunningham, Christie Rigg, Walter Warner, John Larimore, and two partnership experts for suggestions for improvements to the second edition—Roger Pritchard, a Berkeley, California, small business adviser, and Attorney Elisse Brown of Oakland. And maniacal thanks to our favorite sharp-penciled accountants: Margo Miller of San Francisco, tax expert for small business owners; Bernard "Bear" Kamoroff, author of *Small Time Operator*; and Malcolm Roberts, Berkeley, another tax wiz.

About the Author

Denis Clifford is an estate planning attorney in Berkeley, California. He is the author of many Nolo titles, including *Quick & Legal Will Book*, *Make Your Own Living Trust*, and *Plan Your Estate*. He has been interviewed by such major media as the *New York Times*, *Los Angeles Times*, and *Money Magazine*.

Table of Contents

Appendixes

Introduction to Forming a Partnership

If you are thinking about going into business with a friend, or two, or several, you've come to the right place. If you decide to go into business together, you'll need a legal agreement governing how your shared ownership works. This is no mere formality. It goes to the core of your business: how decisions will be made, how you'll get paid, how you'll work together, and what happens if a partner wants to leave.

Shared owners truly are in it together. The business actions of one owner affect all the others. It's true that "in unity there is strength," which is why going into business with others can be so desirable and beneficial. You can share each other's ideas, enthusiasm, expertise, and financial resources. But with a shared-ownership business, where "all for one and one for all" is the reality, you and your partners will be in trouble if you can't agree on basic issues. *Form a Partnership* explains the essential operational and legal issues that come up when creating a shared-ownership business. Using this book, you can work through these issues and decide how you want to handle them—which will help all of you make sure that you're on the same page and really want to go into business together.

The easiest and cheapest legal form for a shared business is a partnership. This book guides you through each step of creating a legal agreement with your partners, and provides various clauses you can use in your partnership agreement to cover each major issue—from allocating profits and losses to adding a new partner to handling disputes or even dissolving the partnership. With this book, you will be able to create your own partnership agreement tailored to your needs, clause by clause, that you can use for your partnership.

Most people buy this book because they want a nuts-and-bolts guide to forming a partnership. It's also useful for those of you who already have a partnership agreement, but want ideas for updating it (for example, by adding a new clause regarding buyouts).

TIP ICON

Have any doubts as to whether a partnership is right for your shared business? Be sure to read Chapter 1, which walks you through the pros and cons of forming a partnership versus alternative business structures, such as a corporation or an LLC.

Get Updates, Forms, and More Online

You can download any of the forms in this book at:

www.nolo.com/back-of-book/PART.html

See Appendix B for complete instructions on how to download and use the electronic forms. All the forms in this book are also included in Appendix C.

Is a Partnership Right for You?

I f you're considering going into business with a friend, or several friends (or colleagues), you're joining in a basic American dream—running your own show, being your own boss, and hopefully gaining some control over your economic destiny.

Before you take the plunge, however, you should take a step back and consider whether forming a partnership makes sense. We mean this in two ways. First, are you ready to start a shared business of any kind? While there are great benefits to shared ownership, it can also create stress—and it will definitely require you to work very closely with your co-owners. Before you get started, it makes good sense to take a very close look at your own willingness to be that intimately involved with your prospective partners.

Second, if you decide that you want to start a shared-ownership business, what legal form should that business take? A partnership is only one of several ways you can structure a shared-ownership business. Before you invest the time and energy drafting a partnership agreement, you should carefully consider whether another ownership structure—such as a corporation or a limited liability company—might better suit your business.

This chapter will help you answer both questions. If you decide, after careful consideration, that forming a partnership is the best way to realize your business and personal goals, the rest of this book will take you step-by-step through drafting a partnership agreement that will serve your business well for years to come.

Sharing Ownership of a Business

The advantages of having one or more co-owners can be tremendous, but so can the headaches of trying to make group decisions, agree on business goals, run your company together, and distribute the work, profits, and debt fairly. Whether shared ownership is right for you depends both on your own personality and on the partners you've chosen.

Advantages and Drawbacks

Shared ownership has many benefits. The chemistry and spirit of two, three, or more minds working together can often produce exciting results. There's more energy and enthusiasm, and—at least as important—more cash, skills, and resources. And it's a lot easier to arrange for time off if you have partners than if you're trying to run a business all by yourself.

But for all of those who dream of doing their own thing—and who hasn't?—only a relatively small number will be committed enough to invest the love and labor necessary to get a small business off the ground. Those who do will almost inevitably go through periods of stress, and their survival will depend on their ability to quickly and competently master all sorts of unfamiliar skills and tasks. In a partnership business, there are also the stresses and risks that can come with shared ownership. Money can be incendiary stuff. Before you decide to throw in your financial lot with others, you need to make sure you're willing and able to become involved that intimately with each other.

In a shared business, your co-owners will make decisions that directly affect your life. Of course, there are steps you can take to put some limits on this, such as requiring decisions to be made by the whole group or limiting the authority of one owner to act for others. But ultimately, sharing a business requires you to give up some control. Shared ownership allows you to share the burdens of your business, but it also requires you to share the responsibilities. If that doesn't sound like you, a shared-ownership business probably isn't the right call.

Choosing the Right Partners

The most important assets of any shared business are the co-owners' competence, determination to work hard, and the trust they have in one another. Of course, your business partners must share your dream, but they must also be willing to share the work. Of course, you and your partners should get along well personally, but that's not enough. You must also have compatible work styles, have similar expectations about how much each of you will do for the business, and have the same goals for your business's future.

Partnerships are (very) human enterprises. While we can't tell you exactly who you should pick as a partner, we can tell you that not every friendship—or every romantic relationship—makes a good business partnership. Our experience has taught us that there are a few questions prospective partners should consider before throwing in their lot with one another:

- Do you all understand and agree that you're going to run a business with the aim of making a decent profit? Any money-making enterprise qualifies as a business. If any would-be partners are nonbusiness types who simply aren't comfortable with that, you (and they) don't want to be part of the same partnership.
- How long have you known each other? We've seen some new friendships crumble under the stress of running a business together. Don't enter any partnership casually.
- Are all prospective partners roughly on the same economic footing? If not, how do you feel about the possibility that some partners' decisions may be based not on the business's economic realities, but on their own outside financial resources or needs?
- How's your chemistry? There are no rules at all here. Sometimes, people with different temperaments work out very well as partners. And sometimes, people who are longtime friends with very similar personalities can't develop a harmonious business relationship. Probably, the best you can do is ask yourself whether you can imagine being in a close business relationship with your prospective partners ten or more years from now. If you can't, think twice about going forward.

Business Structure Options

There are five common legal forms of business ownership:

- partnership
- sole proprietorship

- corporation
- limited liability company, and
- limited partnership.

Some states have distinct subcategories of these five, especially partnerships. For example, there's a creature called a "mining partnership" used for mining and oil ventures in some states. In this chapter, we'll just concern ourselves with the basic forms.

To help you choose the business structure that best suits your needs, this chapter explains the legal and practical consequences of each option. Of course, our emphasis is on the partnership form, but don't assume that it must be the right one for you without exploring your alternatives. We've received letters from readers of earlier editions telling us that after reading these materials, they decided to form a small corporation or a sole proprietorship. That's great; the time to consider your options is here at the start. Once you've created your legal form, it takes some time and trouble to change it.

Partnerships

In this section, we give you a quick look at the nature of partnerships, so that you can compare them to corporations, limited liability companies, and sole proprietorships. Later in this chapter, we'll explore the partnership legal form in more depth.

Here are five key points about partnerships:

1. A partnership is a business owned by two or more people.
2. Each partner can perform all acts that are necessary to operate the business, including hiring employees and spending or borrowing money. (However, you can put some limits on a partner's authority, as explained in "A Closer Look at Partnerships," below.) Each partner is personally liable for all debts incurred by the business. This is a vital reason why your partners must be trustworthy. If a creditor has a claim against your partnership and the partnership doesn't have enough assets to satisfy that claim, the personal assets of any partner can be taken to pay the business debts.

3. Partners share in profits or losses, in whatever proportion they've agreed on. Partnerships themselves don't pay taxes (although they do file an annual tax form). The partners report their share of profits or losses on their individual tax returns, as part of their regular income.

4. Partnerships begin when two or more people form a business. Although technically a partnership ends if one partner leaves, you can agree at the beginning that the partnership business will continue to be run by the remaining partners, if there are any. If you want the business to continue after a partner leaves—and almost all partnerships work this way—you'll need to work out what will happen to the interest of the departing partner. Who can, or must, buy that interest? How will you determine a fair price for that interest? (See Chapter 5.)

5. The owners should have a written partnership agreement specifying their respective rights and responsibilities. Preparing this agreement is at the heart of this book. The purpose of a partnership agreement is to cover all major issues that may affect the partnership, from the manner of dividing profits and losses to management of the business to buyout provisions in case a partner leaves or dies. This agreement does not have to be filed with any government agency, and no official approval is required to start the partnership.

Sole Proprietorships

A sole proprietor means, as the words say, that there's one owner of the business. The owner may hire (and fire) employees. The owner may even arrange for employees to receive a percentage of the business profits as part of their wages, but he or she remains the sole owner. The owner—and the owner alone—is personally liable for all the debts, taxes, and liabilities of the business, including claims made against employees acting in the course and scope of their employment. The business does not pay taxes as an entity; instead, the owner reports and pays taxes on the profits of the business on his or her own individual income tax returns.

RESOURCE

Want more information on setting up and running a sole proprietorship? Take a look at *The Small Business Start-Up Kit*, by Peri Pakroo, *Legal Guide for Starting & Running a Small Business*, by Fred S. Steingold, or *The Women's Small Business Start-Up Kit*, by Peri Pakroo, all by Nolo.

Personality Traits and the Sole Proprietorship

Quite simply, the main advantage of a sole proprietorship is that there is only one boss (you), so potential managerial conflicts are eliminated, except for your inner ones. The disadvantages stem from the source— there is only you as owner and boss. If you get sick, want time off, or simply want to share the responsibility of decision making with someone else, you won't have a lot of flexibility.

Whether you should be the only boss is often a question of temperament. Some people like, and need, to run the whole show and always chafe in a shared ownership situation, while others want, need, or at least appreciate the resources and strengths, from cash to camaraderie, that co-owners can bring. The best advice we can give you here is that old axiom—know thyself.

Sole Proprietorship Compared With Shared Ownership

In deciding whether to operate a business as a sole proprietorship or adopt a form of shared ownership such as a partnership, a business organizer may be inclined to choose shared ownership to involve key employees in the future of the business. While it may make great sense to allow important employees to become co-owners, either as partners or stockholders, this is not the only way to reward dedicated and talented employees. A profit-sharing agreement within the framework of the sole proprietorship may be a good alternative approach, at least until you see if you and the key employees are compatible over the long term.

Terminating a Sole Proprietorship

When the owner dies, a sole proprietorship ends. By contrast, in theory at least, a partnership, a small corporation, or a limited liability company can continue under the direction of the surviving owners. Practically, however, a sole proprietor who wants his or her business to continue after its owner dies can leave the remaining assets (after paying off its debts, of course) to someone who will continue its operations.

> **CAUTION**
>
> **Sole proprietors need to plan for probate.** If the owner of a sole proprietorship leaves business assets through the owner's will, the probate process can take up to a year and make it difficult for the inheritors to either operate or sell the business (or any of its assets). To avoid this, small business owners should consider transferring the business into a living trust, a legal device which avoids probate and allows the assets to be transferred to the inheritors promptly. (For more information on creating a living trust for a business, see *Plan Your Estate*, by Denis Clifford (Nolo).)

Corporations

A corporation is a legal entity separate from its owners, who are its shareholders. Traditionally, the chief attraction of running a small business as a corporation is that the shareholder owners enjoy limited personal liability for business debts or obligations. Ordinarily, each shareholder stands to lose only what he or she has invested in the corporation. Other assets, such as the owners' houses and investments, can't be grabbed to pay business debts.

A corporation is created by filing articles of incorporation with the appropriate state agency, usually the secretary or department of state. Unlike partnerships, sole proprietorships, and LLCs, corporations must also hold formal director and shareholder meetings and document major corporate decisions in corporate minutes. If corporations don't hold these meetings or prepare records of these corporate decisions, the owners risk losing their limited liability. Instead of a partnership agreement, corporations have bylaws that establish the organization's internal governing rules.

Corporations are taxed first at the business entity level and, then again, when corporate owners pay personal income tax on corporate profits distributed to them. But this double taxation can be minimized or avoided if the owners pay out profits to themselves as tax-deductible salaries and benefits.

For many new owners of small businesses, immediately forming a corporation isn't necessary. Usually, the corporate form of doing business provides no real advantage over a partnership or limited liability company and sometimes can be disadvantageous. And remember, whichever legal ownership form you decide upon, you'll have to resolve the same basic issues regarding power between the owners.

Limited Liability Companies

Limited liability companies (LLCs) attempt to blend many of the benefits of a partnership and a corporation. The business can choose to be treated as a partnership, taxwise, which means all profits are taxed at the individual level rather than the business level. But LLCs also permit owners to obtain a key attraction of a corporation—limited liability. An LLC owner's personal assets cannot be taken to pay business debts. And, LLCs are generally not required to observe the same formalities as a corporation—they don't have to elect directors, hold annual shareholders meetings, or even prepare formal minutes of meetings or business decisions, unless they agree to do so in writing.

To form an LLC, the owners prepare articles of organization which include basic facts, such as the LLC's name, principal office address, agent and office for receiving legal papers, and the names of the initial owners. An LLC's articles of organization must be filed with the appropriate state agency, usually the department or secretary of state's office. Most states require an LLC to file an annual form or report. A number of states impose annual fees on LLCs and a few impose annual franchise taxes. In California, for example, LLCs must pay a minimum annual fee of $800.

Business Structures for Professionals

Some professions are regulated by state law and cannot use simple, ordinary partnerships. For example, under almost all states' laws, doctors cannot form general partnerships. Other health care professionals—dentists, nurses, opticians, optometrists, pharmacists, and physical therapists—are similarly regulated. So are some other professions, normally including psychologists, accountants, engineers, and veterinarians. The scope and details of regulation vary from state to state.

However, laws in every state permit shared ownership by regulated professionals using different business structures. They can form a "professional corporation" or a "professional service corporation," and, in some states, a "professional limited liability company." Also, in some states, certain types of partnerships are allowed, sometimes called "limited liability partnerships." If you are in a regulated profession, see a lawyer.

Whatever legal form a shared professional business takes, the owners must resolve the same basic questions that are involved in setting up a partnership: who contributes what, how work is allocated, how profits are shared, and what happens if an owner leaves. Though you'll eventually need a lawyer to prepare the formal ownership documents, you'll benefit by working through these issues yourselves, before seeking legal help.

Like a partnership, an LLC also should have a written agreement (called an "operating agreement"), which defines the basic rights and responsibilities of the LLC owners. To prepare a sound operating agreement, LLC owners must deal with the same issues as partners preparing a partnership agreement, including how much capital each member will contribute to get the business going, how much each person will work for the business, to whom departing members can sell their share of the business, and how that share is to be valued.

RESOURCE

If you want to create a limited liability company. You can form your LLC online with Nolo's Online LLC (available at www.nolo.com) or you can find all the forms and information you need to create your own LLC in *Form Your Own Limited Liability Company,* by Anthony Mancuso (Nolo).

Like shareholders of a corporation, the owners of an LLC generally are not liable for company debts beyond the amount each has invested in the company. However, unlike a corporation, an LLC is not subject to income tax as a business entity unless its owners choose to be taxed this way. Usually, owners choose to be treated like a partnership for tax purposes with LLC profits "flowing through" to the owners, meaning that usually any profits the business earns are subject to federal income tax only on the owner's personal tax return.

For most small businesses organized as LLCs, the owners are also the managers of the business. However, an LLC can also be used as a type of investment device, in which many or even most owners do not take an active role in business management but instead are passive investors. The business is run by a small group of the owners, called a "management group" or "board of managers." In this type of LLC, the manager-owners must comply with federal and state securities laws when selling interests in the LLC to passive investors. To be sure you know how to comply with the securities laws, you must do careful legal research yourself or see a securities lawyer.

Converting a Partnership to an LLC

It's fully legal to change the structure of a business from a partnership to an LLC at any time. Essentially, the LLC articles of organization that you must create and file to convert a partnership are the same as those required to create an LLC from scratch. The partnership agreement, perhaps with minor technical modifications, can be renamed the LLC operating agreement. Once a partnership has been converted into an LLC, the owners have limited liability for all future business debts and obligations. The creation of the LLC does not, however, wipe out the owners' (the former partners') responsibility for any *previous* partnership debts or obligations.

Limited Partnerships

A limited partnership is a special kind of legal animal that, in some circumstances, combines the best attributes of a partnership and a corporation. Its advantage as a business structure is that it provides a way for business owners to raise money without having to give up managerial control or go to the trouble of creating a corporation and issuing stock.

A limited partnership must have at least one general partner, the person or entity that really runs things. The general partner can be another partnership, an LLC, a corporation, or a human being. There can also be more than one general partner. However many there are, each general partner has the rights and potential liabilities normally involved in any partnership—such as management powers for the business and personal liability for business losses or debts.

Limited partners, on the other hand, have no management powers, but neither are they personally liable for the debts of the partnership. Limited partners are basically investors. The return they receive for their investment is defined in the partnership agreement. If the business fails, the most that the limited partners can lose is what they invested in the business. Limited partners can also be a useful means to raise money for expanding an existing business, especially at times when other sources of cash are tight and interest rates are high.

CAUTION

Limited partnership interests are securities. Offering and selling limited partnership interests involves the sale of what's called a security. The most common example of a security is a corporate stock or bond. You must comply with all the applicable federal and state securities laws when you offer any limited partnership interest for sale.

Legal Formalities of Limited Partnerships

Limited partnerships involve many more legal formalities than general partnerships. In addition to securities laws, limited partnerships are generally subject to other state controls. Setting up and operating a limited partnership is similar in many ways to the process of organizing and operating a small corporation. State law usually requires that a registration certificate be filed with a government agency. The information required on this document varies, depending on state law. Often, partnership and limited partnership agreements must be disclosed, and the names and addresses of all partners and limited partners listed. Failure to comply with state registration requirements can subject the partner-ship to serious penalties and cause would-be limited partners to lose their limited liability status.

Restrictions on Limited Partnerships

State law normally imposes restrictions on the availability and use of limited partnership names. In addition, these laws govern the manner of calling and holding meetings and may impose many other legal requirements, which apply to the operation of the limited partnership unless alternative rules are clearly spelled out in the partnership agreement.

! CAUTION

This book does not enable you to prepare a limited partnership yourself. This book does not include sample clauses for actually drafting a limited partnership agreement. One reason for this is that each state's laws governing limited partnerships mandate technical legal requirements that must be met to establish a valid limited partnership. You should consult with an attorney for help creating a limited partnership.

Comparing Partnerships to LLCs and Corporations

No matter which legal form you and your co-owners choose, you must confront and resolve the same day-to-day problems, such as allocating shares of ownership, operating the business, paying salaries and profits, and resolving disputes, among others. One obvious advantage of forming a partnership is that you don't have to pay costly filing and other fees, as you would to form a corporation or an LLC. But, overall, for many business owners the advantages and disadvantages of these three ways to organize your business are not as significant as many advocates of one or the other approach would have you believe.

For example, suppose you and two friends are co-owners of a computer repair business. It's clearly prudent to decide what will happen if one person unexpectedly quits or dies. A common method of handling this is to create a "buyout" clause, enabling the remaining owners to purchase (usually over time) the interest of the departing owner. If the business is owned as a partnership, the buyout clause you devise will normally be included in the partnership agreement. If the business is an LLC, the clause will be in the owners' operating agreement. In a corporation, this clause is normally put in the bylaws or in a shareholders' agreement. But the practical reality will be the same.

Below we look in depth at key issues concerning the form of ownership of a shared business. We'll start here by summarizing the most important points:

- The partnership form is the simplest and least expensive of the three forms to create and maintain.
- For small, shared-ownership businesses that face the risk of significant lawsuits or want to avoid personal liability exposure for their owners, the LLC is usually the best initial choice.
- For other types of small shared-ownership businesses, the partnership form is often the best choice. If business growth makes a different structure more desirable, the partners can easily convert to an LLC or a corporation.
- Occasionally, the corporate form makes sense for a new business. For instance, a corporation may be desirable if the owners want to raise large sums of money from a number of investors.

RESOURCE

Want more information on other business structures? In this book about partnerships, the discussion of other ways to organize your business is necessarily limited. For a more in-depth discussion of the pros and cons of sole proprietorships, LLCs, and corporations, see *Legal Guide for Starting & Running a Small Business*, by Fred S. Steingold (Nolo), and *LLC or Corporation?* by Anthony Mancuso (Nolo). You may also be able to get help from state government sources.

Limited Liability

Shareholders of an LLC or a corporation are not normally personally liable for corporate debts or liability stemming from lawsuits, as long as the LLC or corporation is adequately capitalized (that is, it has sufficient cash or other assets invested). This is called "limited liability." In partnerships, all partners have open-ended personal liability for all partnership debts. But before you rush to form an LLC or incorporate, you should know that the difference between limited and unlimited liability is often less significant than many people believe.

There are two important forms of liability almost any business must deal with: lawsuits and business debts.

Lawsuits

Most small business people with common sense, whether incorporated or not, purchase insurance to protect themselves from the most obvious sorts of liability claims (such as insurance protecting restaurant owners from claims filed by customers who become ill or fall down in the premises). An LLC or a corporation's limited liability is obviously no substitute for business liability insurance, since limited liability doesn't protect the assets of the LLC or corporation itself from being wiped out by a successful claim. However, limited liability can be a valuable protection if a small business is engaged in a high-risk activity and insurance coverage is unavailable or too expensive.

Many American businesses, including many retailers and small service providers, do not normally face serious risk of liability stemming from their business (aside from things like vehicle accidents, which obviously can and should be covered by insurance). For instance, businesses as varied as a shoe store, a graphic design outfit, a small publishing company, or an ice cream parlor are unlikely to face a lawsuit for large sums of money. By contrast, other types of business—for instance, manufacturers or businesses that handle toxic materials—have a much higher risk of liability claims. And because they do, it's often prohibitively expensive for the owners of these types of businesses to purchase insurance to cover potential lawsuit judgments. Some other types of high-risk businesses include:

- **Accountants.** There have been some huge, successful claims against accounting firms for negligence. In some of these situations, accountants were found to be liable when they helped businesses conceal large losses or other damaging financial facts, thus costing investors and suppliers millions.
- **Lawyers.** Law firms can also face immense financial exposure for negligent, or worse, conduct. This conduct can range from actively participating in, or at least negligently abetting, fraudulent behavior by a client to causing financial injury to the law firm's own client.
- **Architects and Construction Companies.** In the day of multimillion-dollar judgments for injured persons and frequent problems with cost overruns, everyone in the construction field is vulnerable to suit for all sorts of reasons.
- **Real Estate.** Increasingly, buyers of property who later discover undisclosed defects—everything from termites, water in the basement, land shifting, or a nasty next-door neighbor—sue both the seller and the real estate people who represent the seller.

This list is intended to be instructive, not exhaustive. We can't give you definitive advice about the liability/lawsuit risks of the type of business you plan to engage in. Only you can decide how serious these risks are and what kinds of steps you can sensibly take to eliminate or at least minimize them. The higher the risk, the more desirable the LLC or corporation. And, obviously, the lower the risks, the more a partnership agreement, combined with basic liability insurance (such as for "slip and fall" accidents on the business premises) and vehicle insurance, should safely protect you.

Debts

What about debts? If the business loses money, as lots of new ventures do, doesn't limited liability protect individual owners from having personal assets taken as part of an LLC or corporate bankruptcy or liquidation? Again, while the answer is "yes" in theory, in reality limited liability protection is likely to be immaterial. Why? Because lenders and major creditors are well aware of the rules of limited owner liability. Banks, landlords, and other savvy businesspeople routinely require the owners of a new small business (whether a partnership, an LLC, or a corporation) to personally guarantee any loan or significant extension of credit made to the business. By doing this, LLC or corporate owners put themselves on much the same legal footing with their creditors as if they ran their business as a partnership. However, we should note that because many providers of routine business supplies and services do not require a personal guarantee from LLC or corporation owners, these owners can escape personal liability for these types of debts if the business becomes insolvent.

Here's another important restriction on the limited liability of corporate and LLC owners: A corporation or LLC must start with a minimally reasonable amount of cash ("capital") to function in the business world. If the entity is only a shell, without the cash necessary to function, a court may "pierce the corporate veil" and hold individual corporate or LLC owners personally responsible for all the entity's debts, whether they personally guaranteed them or not. While it is fairly rare for a court to determine that a corporation or LLC was undercapitalized, it can happen, particularly if fraud is involved.

Business Continuity

Corporations have "eternal life." This means that if one (or even all) of the principal owners of a small corporation dies, the corporate entity continues to exist. Partnerships, on the other hand, can dissolve when any partner withdraws or dies. However, this difference is also immaterial in real life. It's easy, and fully legal, to insert a standard clause in your partnership agreement that provides that the partnership entity continues after one owner leaves or dies.

LLCs are often functionally similar to partnerships regarding business continuity. Some state statutes require members of an LLC to vote to continue the LLC within a specified period of time after a member withdraws or dies; if they do not, the LLC is technically dissolved. Many LLC operating agreements provide that an owner's departure triggers a vote by the remaining owners on whether to continue the LLC. The effect is that, if the owners wish it, the LLC will continue in business without legal interruption.

> **CAUTION**
>
> **A general partnership isn't the right choice if you want to raise money from people who won't participate in the business.** For larger businesses that need to raise money from outside investors and will comply with complicated federal and state securities registration and sales laws to do so, it can sometimes be psychologically easier to raise capital by selling stock to passive investors than by trying to sell participation in a partnership. This will constitute a limited partnership, though, instead of a general partnership.

Transfer of Ownership

Corporate ownership comes in the form of shares that can theoretically be transferred to new owners. By contrast, a partner's interest cannot be transferred without the consent of all partners except when, as is rarely the case, the partnership agreement expressly allows for free transferability. Similarly, an owner of an LLC is usually restricted by state law or the members' operating agreement (or both) from transferring an ownership interest in the business without the consent of all other owners. But does this legal difference really add up to a practical difference?

The answer is no, for two reasons. First, when it comes to small, closely held corporations, state law often restricts the right of a shareholder to freely transfer shares no matter what the shareholders want. Second, the stock of most small corporations is extremely difficult or even impossible to sell. There is no regular, public market for small business interests.

In addition, the bylaws or shareholders' agreement of many small corporations—just like the partnership agreements of most partnerships and operating agreements of LLCs—restrict the right of any owner to sell to a third person and provide that the remaining owners have the option to buy out the interest of any departing owner. So again, the realities of running a small business dictate that the owners take certain similar steps to limit or prevent sales to outside buyers, no matter what the legal form of the business.

Business Formalities

No state or federal law or agency requires a partnership to file its original agreement or maintain any ongoing paperwork. By contrast, government paperwork and costs are required to start up an LLC or a corporation. A corporation and an LLC must file their organizational documents with the secretary or department of state. The costs for these initial filings are modest in most states—typically $100 or so. Some states impose yearly fees or franchise taxes which can be more substantial ($800 in California).

Once it's operational, an LLC generally does not have to observe the same formalities as a corporation (such as holding annual meetings) but can mostly function with the informality of a partnership. Like a partnership, an LLC can function with exactly the amount of formality—formal meetings, quorum requirements, keeping minutes of meetings, and so on—that the owners want. Most states do, however, require LLCs to file a brief annual report, in addition to any fees or taxes imposed.

RESOURCE

Resources to incorporate your business. Nolo publishes three books (all by Anthony Mancuso) that can significantly reduce the cost of creating and maintaining a corporation:

- *How to Form Your Own California Corporation.* Contains excellent information and forms for creating a corporation in California.
- *Incorporate Your Business: A Step-by-Step Guide to Forming a Corporation in Any State.* Useful for all states.
- *The Corporate Records Handbook: Meetings, Minutes & Resolutions.* Provides all the forms and information corporations in any state need to properly document ongoing business matters.

Taxation

A partnership is not taxed. Partnership net income (profits) is taxed only on the individual partners' income tax returns. An LLC can choose to be taxed as a partnership or as a small corporation. Most LLCs choose to be taxed in the same way as partnerships.

You might think that partnerships and LLCs enjoy a real advantage over corporations because corporate profits are taxed twice (first at the corporate level and then at the shareholder level), while partnership or LLC income is only taxed once. For small businesses, this distinction usually is immaterial. Small corporations can often avoid double taxation. They can pay out to owners most of what would otherwise be corporate profits in the form of salaries, bonuses, and other fringe benefits (rather than in dividends). As long as the owners actually work in the business and the salaries aren't outrageously unreasonable, paying the owners salaries as employees is acceptable to the IRS. Because monies paid in salaries, bonuses, Social Security, health plans, and other fringe benefits are deductible business expenses for the corporation, these expenses are not subject to corporate tax. In this way, many small corporations reduce their corporate income to zero, and corporate income is taxed only at the individual level.

In some situations, corporate taxation allows small business people to pay less overall tax on their income by retaining a portion of corporate or LLC profits in the corporation from one year to the next. The individual shareholder-owner is taxed only on income received, whether in the form of corporate salary or as profits. The profits retained by the corporation or LLC are also taxed, but at a generally lower rate. A corporation can retain accumulated earnings up to $250,000 without tax. Any retained earnings above $250,000 are taxed at a 20% rate.

In a partnership or an LLC that has chosen to be taxed like a partnership, these retained profits would be taxed as income to the partners at their marginal rate, which will probably be much higher, whether or not they actually received any cash. For businesses that will pay all profits to owner-employees in the form of salaries and benefits, these initial low rates of corporate taxation offer no advantage. However, if your business will need to retain substantial earnings for future operations, incorporating is likely to make economic sense. While corporations can retain profits of up to $250,000 for future needs, LLCs do not have this right.

Small corporate businesses can also avoid double taxation by electing S corporation status. An S corporation functions like a partnership for income tax purposes. Thus, an S corporation doesn't pay income taxes on profits; only the shareholders do.

Finally, a corporation or an LLC can establish a tax-deductible pension and/or profit-sharing plan for all its workers, including working shareholders and/or managing owners, while a partnership pension plan is only tax deductible for employees, not for partners themselves. However, this difference, too, is often more apparent than real, since partners are eligible for individual profit-sharing retirement plans, which tend to equalize tax treatment.

Termination

When a corporation is dissolved and distributes appreciated property to shareholders, the gain (increase) in value is taxed both to the corporation and to the shareholders. This means that it can potentially be more expensive to close down a profitable corporation than a partnership or an LLC that has elected to be taxed like a partnership.

A Closer Look at Partnerships

The legal definition of a partnership is "an association of two or more persons to carry on as co-owners of a business for profit." (Uniform Partnership Act (UPA) Section 6(1).) You don't have to use the words "partners" or "partnership" to become a legal partnership. If you simply join with other persons and run a shared business, you've created a partnership. Using those words will, however, ensure that your business is treated as a partnership.

Partners and Spouses

Increasingly, couples are running businesses together. IRS statistics indicate that there are well over 800,000 businesses in the United States with ownership shared between spouses.

There is no special IRS category for couple or spouse-owned businesses. Unless another legal form is used, a business co-owned by a couple is simply a partnership.

For more information, search the IRS website. For example, see "Election for Married Couples Unincorporated Businesses," at www.irs.gov/businesses/small-businesses-self-employed/election-for-married-couples-unincorporated-businesses.

Partnership Basics

Here are some basic rules applicable to partnerships.

Oral Partnership Agreements

As a practical matter, partnerships should always have a written partnership agreement. You should know, however, that oral or handshake partnerships are often legal, although highly inadvisable. If there's even a minor disagreement between the partners, it will probably be very hard to prove what the agreement was—or even that the partnership existed.

Equal Versus Unequal Ownership

Partners don't have to share ownership equally. You can agree on any percentage of individual ownership or distribution of the profits that you want. Thus, one partner could own 80% of the partnership and four more could own 5% each.

Professional Partnerships

Partnerships can be organized for all sorts of purposes. They can sell products or services just as they can manufacture, mine, or operate as agents. Professional partnerships, however, such as those of lawyers or doctors, are subject to special rules set down by the state, because of the special licensing and regulation of these professions. Usually the most important rule is that everyone in the partnership be a member of the profession.

Compensation of Partners

Partners don't normally receive salaries per se; usually, they get a percentage of the profits. However, partners often take an agreed-upon amount from the business—commonly called a draw—at regular intervals (for example, monthly, biweekly) against their yearly partnership shares.

Liability

Partners are personally and individually liable for all the legal obligations of the partnership.

Intent to Be Partners

Because partnerships don't have to file any formal paperwork, there can be some confusion as to whether a true legal partnership exists. And, because one partner can bind the others legally, you'll want to be very clear about whether you do—or don't—belong to a partnership.

To create a valid partnership, each person must intend to be a partner. Partners must be volunteers; they can't be drafted against their will. However, the law allows one's intent to be a partner to be implied from the circumstances of a business operation. For example, if three people who have no other business relationship each inherit one-third of some real estate or a business, they don't automatically become partners because they've never agreed to do business together. But if they then proceed to run the business or develop the land together, they've become partners even if there is no written partnership agreement.

Not every active joining of interests makes people partners, either for tax purposes or legally. Here are two examples:

- Mere co-owners of property are not partners, even if they lease the property and share rents, provided they don't actively carry on a business on or with the property.
- Sharing the expense of a project does not automatically create a partnership or joint venture. For example, if two adjoining landowners construct a ditch merely to drain surface waters from their property, there is no partnership for tax purposes.

In general, if a person receives a share of the profits of an (unincorporated) business, it's an indication that the person is a partner in the business. The complexities of business relationships, however, can make this rule tough to apply.

EXAMPLE: Al lends money to Jane and Joan's partnership business. That alone clearly doesn't make him a partner—unless the loan is really a disguised ownership investment in the business. A key factor here is if a definite time is established when the loan is due. If not, the loan looks like an investment. But suppose Al imposes some controls along with his loan (for example, he requires some new inventory controls). Does this render Al actively involved in the management of the business, and hence a partner? The answer is— it might. The IRS takes the position that when a lender imposes "excessive controls" on a loan, he or she becomes a partner. The IRS hasn't defined exactly when controls become "excessive," so be wary.

Joint Ventures (Partnerships for a Single Purpose)

A joint venture is simply a partnership for a limited or specified purpose. If you and Jose go into the construction business together, that's a partnership. If you and Jose agree to build one house together, that's probably a joint venture. Common examples of joint ventures are natural resource projects—drilling for oil or a cooperative mining venture.

Joint ventures are governed by partnership law. The relations of the joint venturers should be defined in a written agreement, just like any partnership. Indeed, except for the fact that the agreement should state that the venture is limited to a specified project, the same issues and problems must be resolved when creating a joint venture agreement as in a partnership agreement.

The Rights and Responsibilities of Partners— Or, One Partner Can Bind Another

Each partner has full power to represent and bind the partnership within the normal course of business. (UPA Section 9.) This is one obvious reason trust is so vital in a partnership. One partner can obligate the other partners, even if they never authorized him or her to do so. Indeed, in many circumstances, a partner can bind a partnership even when the other partners told him or her not to.

> EXAMPLE: Al, Fred, and Mike are partners in a printing business. They discuss buying an expensive new computer and vote two-to-one against it. Fred, the disgruntled loser, goes out and signs a contract for the computer with a company that has no knowledge of Al's and Mike's vehement opposition. Because this is within the normal course of business, Fred's act binds the partnership.

It is legal to limit the powers of any partner in the partnership agreement. (UPA Section 18(3).) However, those limits are unlikely to be binding on people outside the partnership who have no actual knowledge of them. Legally, outsiders are entitled to rely on the apparent authority of a partner, as determined by the customs of the particular trade or business involved or the normal course of (that particular) business. When Fred bought the computer (in the above example), the salesperson—as long as he or she had no actual knowledge of the partnership's limits on Fred—relied on Fred's apparent authority; a partner of a computer printing business can reasonably be expected to have the authority to buy a computer. However, if Fred wanted to bind the computer printing partnership in a deal to open a chain of hair salons, an outsider probably wouldn't be able to rely on his signature alone as binding on the partnership, because this would be outside the normal course of the partnership's business. (For more on a partner's authority to bind the partnership, see Chapter 3.)

Personal Liability for Partnership Debts

Each partner is personally liable for all partnership debts and obligations that the partnership cannot pay. This is not a rule that the partners can change as far as debts to third parties go. Partners are not liable for the personal, nonpartnership debts and obligations of another partner. However, if one partner is having financial problems outside the partnership, creditors can seek to get at that partner's share of the partnership, and this can severely disrupt the business. In addition to business debts, partners are also personally liable for any money damages that result from the negligence of another partner, as well as damages that result from fraud or other intentional acts a partner commits in the ordinary course of partnership business.

EXAMPLE: Jane and Alfonso are partners in a retail flower business. Jane has no money; Alfonso is rich. The partnership just opened, and the partners haven't gotten around to buying insurance yet. While Jane is driving the flower delivery van to pick up flowers on partnership business, she hits and severely injures a pedestrian, who then sues and gets a substantial judgment. Alfonso is personally liable for any amount unpaid by the business—that is, what's left unpaid after all partnership assets have been used. If he doesn't have sufficient cash, or liquid assets, to cover the judgment, his other property, from real estate to cars—with the exception of whatever is protected by state debtors' exemption laws—can be seized to satisfy it.

A silent partner—one whose membership in the partnership is not revealed to the public—is every bit as liable for partnership debts as any other partner. However, a subpartner (sometimes called an assignee) is not. A subpartner or assignee is a person who agrees with one member of a partnership to share in that partner's profits. Although the assignee or subpartner has the right to receive a portion of the partner's profits, he or she does not have any rights or responsibilities as a partner. This is a separate agreement between the partner and the subpartner and does not, legally, involve the subpartner in the partnership. Creating this kind of arrangement can get complicated, so see a lawyer if you're interested in doing this.

Partnerships and Taxes

Partnerships do not pay federal or state income taxes. However, every partnership must file an informational partnership tax return (IRS Form 1065) once a year. Any profits or losses from the partnership flow through the partnership to the individual partners. Thus, only the individual partners pay taxes on partnership profits. (See Chapter 8.)

Unlike corporations, there cannot be double taxation of partnership profits, once at the partnership level and then a second time when partnership profits are distributed to the individual partners. Under the tax code, partners' incomes or losses may be, for IRS purposes, either earned, investment, or passive. Briefly, if all partners materially participate in the operations of the business—which is certainly the rule for most small business partnerships—partners' incomes will be considered earned. As we explain in Chapter 8, it's generally desirable from a tax point of view to have earned income rather than passive or investment income.

Partners' Legal Relation to One Another

Partners are fiduciaries vis-à-vis one another. This bit of legal jargon means that they owe complete loyalty to the partnership and cannot engage in any activity that conflicts with the partnership's business. As one court put it, "The rule of undivided loyalty is relentless and supreme."

> EXAMPLE: Fred and Tom agree to be partners in a real estate purchase. In the course of conducting negotiations for that purchase, Fred learns of another real estate buy, a real bargain. Legally, Fred cannot simply wait until the partnership expires and purchase the second property himself. He has a fiduciary duty to tell Tom any valuable information he learns while acting on partnership business. Similarly, if Fred proposes to buy Tom out of the partnership, he can't legally do so without telling Tom about the bargain he's found. The rule of caveat emptor (let the buyer beware) doesn't apply to a partner. Fred must act in complete good faith, including volunteering any significant information about the partnership, its worth, and business possibilities, which he is aware Tom doesn't know.

There is voluminous litigation on the rights and duties of partners to each other—sad evidence that partnerships can go sour. Here are some representative no-nos, things a partner cannot legally do. Notice that common sense indicates these are not ways in which honest people deal with each other:

- A partner cannot secretly obtain for him- or herself an opportunity available to the partnership.
- Partnership assets cannot be diverted for personal use of the partners.
- Partners cannot fail to distribute partnership profits to other members of the partnership.
- Each partner must disclose any and all material facts affecting the business to the other partners.

CAUTION

Would-be partners beware. The courts have often ruled that those who have seriously discussed forming a partnership must adhere to the same exacting standards of good faith that bind partners, even if they never signed an actual partnership agreement. For example, if two people seriously plan to open a garden nursery and find a perfect location, it's probably a breach of fiduciary duty for one person to try and cut out the other by leasing the place as a sole proprietor. Just when this partnerlike responsibility arises isn't totally clear, but when real negotiating begins, that probably means there are fiduciary duties of trust involved. You'll have to trust your partners eventually, and it makes sense to start building that trust by full disclosure and square dealing right from the start.

Business Start-Up Issues

The technicalities of establishing and maintaining a small business partnership are not unduly burdensome. Once you agree on and create your partnership agreement, that's pretty much it as far as legal paperwork is concerned. You don't have to file any formal papers with any governmental bureau, department, or agency, except that the partnership must file appropriate paperwork with:

- the IRS, to obtain a taxpayer I.D. number, commonly called an "EIN," an Employer Identification Number (IRS Form SS-4)
- the appropriate local agency, if the partnership operates under a fictitious name (a name other than those of the partners). For example, if Wang, Olivier, and Simmons call themselves Ace Electric, they'll have to meet state requirements for all businesses operating under a fictitious name. (See Chapter 3 for more on choosing a business name and fictitious name statements.)

Of course, partnerships have to comply with the same small business and tax paperwork common to any other business. This includes getting a state tax resale permit if they will sell goods, filing payroll and unemployment tax returns if they will hire employees, and generally dealing with all the rest that goes along with starting and operating a business. And, of course, there's internal record keeping, including sales, accounts receivable, general ledger, and other accounting, also required of any business.

Business Resources

Thorough discussions of different aspects of starting and maintaining a small business can be found in the following books:

Legal Guide for Starting & Running a Small Business, by Fred S. Steingold (Nolo). A nuts-and-bolts guide to the laws that affect small businesses every day. The book covers a wide range of important subjects, including leases, trademarks, contracts, franchises, insurance, hiring and firing, and independent contractors.

Legal Forms for Starting & Running a Small Business, by Fred S. Steingold (Nolo). All the forms that small business owners need to handle practical legal problems, from dealing with the IRS to hiring employees and much more.

How to Write a Business Plan, by Mike McKeever (Nolo). This book shows you how to raise money for your new business, including methods for estimating income and raising outside capital by loans or other means. As part of doing this, it forces you to do a thorough financial plan for your proposed business. In our experience, such a plan may demonstrate that even using your best-case assumptions, your proposed business won't produce the financial rewards you expect. In short, this book gives you the tools to reject bad business ideas and refocus on those likely to be profitable.

Deduct It! Lower Your Small Business Taxes, by Stephen Fishman (Nolo). This comprehensive tax deduction guide will help any business save money and make the right tax choices.

Tax Savvy for Small Business, by Frederick W. Daily (Nolo). To run a successful small business, you have to have a good grasp of tax law. This book tells business owners what they need to know about federal taxes and shows them how to make the best tax decisions for their business, maximize profits, and stay out of trouble with the IRS.

The Small Business Start-Up Kit, by Peri Pakroo (Nolo). A user-friendly guide to all major steps involved in launching a new business, including picking a business name, leasing space, preparing an effective business plan, obtaining required licenses and permits, negotiating contracts, managing finances and taxes, marketing your business, and much more.

Business Resources (continued)

The Employer's Legal Handbook, by Fred S. Steingold (Nolo). A comprehensive resource that employers can use for all major employment law concerns, from hiring to firing to everything in between.

Create Your Own Employee Handbook: A Legal & Practical Guide, by Amy DelPo and Lisa Guerin (Nolo). A thorough presentation of how you can create an employee handbook—quickly, easily, and professionally.

Finally, the U.S. Small Business Administration (SBA) website provides extensive information and resources on everything from business finance and management to exporting and franchising. See www.sba.gov for details.

Family Partnerships

The IRS traditionally takes a close look at any partnership involving family members or relations (defined in the Internal Revenue Code, Section 704(e)). Some tax planners tout family limited partnerships as a way to lower income taxes or to shift assets to younger family members free of estate or gift tax. The truth is more complicated. Family limited partnerships can be legal and beneficial in some circumstances. But a family limited partnership must be involved in real business or have a legitimate reason for its existence, unrelated to the tax benefits. They are not valid if they are created solely as a tax scam. Of course, there are many family businesses run as partnerships, including family limited partnerships, that are perfectly legitimate, with several family members active in the business. These partnerships incur no wrath from the IRS.

Terminating a Partnership

In addition to establishing sensible rules for you to follow during the life of your partnership, your partnership agreement governs what will happen if the partnership ends. By termination of a partnership, we mean that the business no longer functions as a partnership. The partnership books are closed, and the partners go their separate ways. One of the other partners may continue the former partnership business in some other form, or, as is probably more common in cases of partnership termination, the business may end as well.

Relationships That Aren't Partnerships

Just as it's important to know what qualifies as a partnership, it can be crucial to recognize a "mock" or "phony" partnership.

Tax Scam Partnerships

Legitimate partnerships, like any other business form, can limit or reduce taxes in some circumstances. However, partnerships are particularly vulnerable to being ruled invalid by the IRS if they are phony relationships designed primarily to lower tax liability.

For example, Daniel and Marie live together. Daniel is a poor artist who makes very little from his paintings; Marie runs a profitable dress store and pays substantial taxes. Can Daniel and Marie legally declare they're now in a partnership to run the dress store and, for tax purposes, each report half the store's profits as their separate incomes, thus lowering their overall tax burden? As you might expect, if the purpose of a partnership is only to evade or reduce taxes, the IRS won't recognize it as a business entity. There must be some genuine sharing, either of management and control of a business or investment in it, for there to be a tax-valid partnership; the partnership can't exist solely in bookkeeping terms. (*IRS v. Tower*, 327 U.S. 290 (1946).)

SEE AN EXPERT

See a lawyer before creating a family limited partnership. These are complex, tricky legal creatures. You need to consult with an attorney to see if one will work for you.

Nonprofit Enterprises

Enterprises not primarily designed to make a profit also fail to qualify as partnerships. Such an endeavor is either a "nonprofit corporation" (if it's incorporated) or an "unincorporated association" (if it isn't). This latter group includes religious, charitable, educational, scientific, civic, social, athletic, and patriotic groups or clubs, and trade unions and associations.

RESOURCE

Want more information about nonprofit corporations? See *How to Form a Nonprofit Corporation*, by Anthony Mancuso (Nolo).

An Overview of Your Partnership Agreement

This chapter looks at the basic elements covered in small business partnership agreements. In Chapters 3 through 6, we discuss these subjects in more detail and provide the specific sample clauses you can use in drafting your partnership agreement.

Good, candid communication is essential to making a partnership work, and that starts at the beginning. Indeed, one of the primary reasons to prepare a written partnership agreement is to make sure the partners agree on important issues—and, if not, to resolve those differences. There's no magic legal formula you can plug in to create a partnership agreement. A lawyer can help you focus on issues and suggest a variety of possible solutions. But no lawyer can make basic choices for you. If you allow a lawyer to decide how your partnership will function, you'll end up with an agreement that is legally impeccable but may not address your real needs.

Preparing Your Agreement

Your situation may require you to alter and revise one or more of the clauses we provide. Or, you may want to cover something we don't discuss, which means you'll have to draft partnership clauses on your own. Be careful here. You do not want any change or new clause to create ambiguity. If you do make significant changes or add new clauses, be sure they clearly express everything all partners have agreed to (and don't contradict anything else in the agreement).

We suggest that you be cautious and selective regarding the amount of detail you include in your partnership agreement. You do need to cover the basics—and you get to decide what those basics are. As tempting as it might be to try, it's never possible to cover every conceivable contingency in your partnership agreement.

Legally, your partnership starts when you agree that it does. In some circumstances, partnerships can be based on an oral agreement or can even be implied from the operational realities of a business. However, the laws of many states effectively compel partnership agreements to be in writing. For example, under New York law, any partnership agreement must be in writing if any of the following applies:

- The agreement is to last for more than one year.
- Real estate is involved.
- An arbitration clause is included.
- There are guaranteed payments to partners.

A written partnership agreement becomes effective when it's signed, unless the agreement itself specifies a different date.

Basic Topics Covered in a Partnership Agreement

The major topics covered in a typical partnership agreement include:

- the authority of a partner
- the name and purpose of the partnership
- contributions to the partnership (cash, property, or services)
- payments from the partnership to the partners (profits, losses, and draws)
- management duties of the partners
- expansion (admission of new partners)
- provisions, in the event a partner dies or withdraws, and
- resolution of disputes (mediation and arbitration).

The Uniform Partnership Act

There's a body of law, primarily the Uniform Partnership Act (UPA) or the Revised Uniform Partnership Act (1997), which establishes some basic legal rules applicable to partnerships.

All but a few of your state's UPA or Revised UPA rules can be varied, if you decide to do so, by an express statement in the partnership agreement. Even if you know your state's UPA rules and decide they are what you want, it is not wise to rely on the UPA to define key issues for your partnership. You should create those clauses yourself and express your decision explicitly in your agreement.

The Uniform Partnership Act or Revised UPA

One of these acts has been adopted in all states except Louisiana. In most states, however, there are some variations, usually slight, between most states' partnership acts and the original uniform act. Uniform acts, as the name indicates, are standardized laws created by a legal commission. However, when it adopts a uniform law, a state legislature can make changes in the uniform version.

The legal citation for each state's UPA or Revised UPA law is set forth in a chart in Appendix A. With basic legal research skills you can use this citation to find your state's laws online or in a local law library.

Joint Ventures

A joint venture is a partnership for a specific limited purpose, such as building one house or giving one series of dance performances. People involved in joint ventures should also have an agreement covering the basics of the partnership and some additional matters, including:

- extent of the venture
- staffing and control of hiring
- conflicts of interest
- management control, and
- tax issues.

Partners: Their Authority and Relationship

The first and most important decision you'll make in organizing your business will be choosing your partners. Once you've done that, you need to set down in your partnership agreement exactly how you'll work together and how each partner will work for the partnership.

Authority of a Partner

The rights and responsibilities of partners can be defined in your partnership agreement with any degree of specificity you desire. Indeed, some partnership agreements contain pages and pages defining the authority, duties, and restrictions on partners. However, this type of endless detail is usually not helpful. In fact, one or more partners' insistence on this approach can signal serious mistrust between the partners. Remember, trust is the central ingredient in any partnership, and no legal clause can compensate for its absence. If you have so little trust in your prospective partners as to think pages of detailed clauses defining the partners' authority are necessary, you should seriously question whether creating a partnership with these people is advisable at all.

Unless the partners decide otherwise, any partner can bind the partnership by decisions made in the ordinary course of partnership business.

> EXAMPLE: Herb, Frank, and Connie are partners in a musical instrument store. Herb, who loves classic rock and roll, orders 36 top-of-the-line Fender Stratocaster electric guitars, far more than the store manages to sell. Herb didn't consult Frank and Connie before ordering the guitars. If he had, they wouldn't have allowed Frank to order so many. Nevertheless, the partnership, and each partner, is liable for the bill for all the guitars.

While the partners' duties to each other are primarily controlled by the partnership agreement, that's not necessarily true for other people dealing with a partner. After all, outsiders usually don't have any idea what's in the partnership agreement. So, in the above example, even if Herb, Frank, and Connie's partnership agreement specifically limited the number or type of electric guitars a partner could commit the partnership to buy, an outsider wouldn't be bound by this unless he or she knew about it. An outsider can legally rely on the "apparent" authority of a partner, as demonstrated by the partner in the course of the business or as typically granted partners in similar business partnerships.

Partnership Decision Making

What is the authority of the partners between themselves to make decisions about normal partnership business? The short answer is that partners may make decisions in any way they agree upon. Often, decision making is done democratically: one partner, one vote. The UPA provides that each partner has an equal vote, even if the partners haven't contributed equal assets to the partnership, but this can be altered in the partnership agreement. We usually recommend this one-partner, one-vote approach because it's more likely to promote harmony and goodwill among the partners. However, some situations—or some people—call for a different approach. How you decide to structure voting power in your partnership isn't a mechanical matter. Rather, it is a reflection of how the partners feel about each other and what each is actually contributing.

Many partnerships have only two partners. Others have a larger even number of partners. Obviously, in these partnerships, there's a possibility of deadlock under a one-partner, one-vote rule, so you'll need to take special care regarding dispute resolution methods. (See Chapter 6.) In theory, having an unequal number of partners eliminates the possibility of deadlock. In the real world, however, you can't avoid a serious conflict just by having an odd number of partners. If the three majority members of a partnership consistently outvote the two minority members, the partnership is likely to be in deep trouble. And it's no help that it got into the mess democratically.

EXAMPLE: Stephanie, Alison, and Lori decide to set up a consulting business. Stephanie contributes $20,000 to start the business and will work full time. Alison contributes $10,000 and will work only occasionally at the business. Lori contributes only $500 and will work half time. Obviously, Stephanie is contributing the most to the business. Should she nevertheless have just one vote, only one-third control in the partnership? That's up to the three partners.

If Stephanie insists she doesn't want to risk being outvoted by the two other partners, and they agree, here are two possible approaches to solve the problem:

- The partnership agreement can provide that each partner's vote is in proportion to her contribution of the partnership capital. This approach leaves Lori without any significant say in the management of the business, because she contributed such a small amount of capital. It might well be fairer to proportion voting rights according to each partner's share of profits, since they (presumably) will reflect contributions of services as well as initial capital to the partnership.
- Another approach is for the partners to agree on what proportion of voting power each partner should receive. For example, the partners could agree that Stephanie will have 60% of the voting power, with Alison and Lori each receiving 20% (and decisions to be made by majority).

Note that both methods leave Stephanie in complete control. Although her problem has been solved, if she ever adopts policies that Alison and Lori don't care for, there's little they can do but resign and try to liquidate the partnership. This isn't easy to do, even if, as we urge, specific clauses have been included in the partnership agreement covering what happens if any partner leaves. (See Chapter 5.) Another approach that can work well for small partnerships is to require that all major decisions be unanimous—that is, every partner has veto power.

As you can see, deciding on a clause involving the control and management of a partnership can be tricky. Sometimes partners try to handle this by going into great detail about how, when, and who makes decisions—down to specifying when meetings will occur and what types of issues must be decided by all partners. We believe a more commonsense approach is to require that major decisions be made and voted on by all partners, with less formal requirements for minor decisions.

Silent Partners

The term "silent partner" can refer to a partner whose involvement isn't revealed to the public, or a partner who contributes only cash to the business and won't work in it, or both. In either case, we advise you to be exceedingly wary when considering having a silent partner as part of your partnership. Indeed, we think it is rarely a good idea, and we urge you to see a knowledgeable lawyer and review your situation carefully before going through with it.

What's troublesome about a silent partner? If a partner's involvement won't be revealed to the public, the question at once arises: Why this secrecy? There's rarely a valid reason for it. Regardless of what is revealed to the public, if the silent partner will contribute only cash to the business, this creates inherent conflicts. The other partners are working, usually very hard, to keep the business alive, while the silent partner isn't. Yet, as a full-fledged owner, the silent partner is entitled to a share of profit of the business and has an equity share of the business. If the business prospers because of the work of the other partners, they're likely to become increasingly resentful of the silent partner. Also, from the silent partner's point of view, he or she has potentially unlimited liability for partnership debts but may not even know about them because of his or her absence from the business.

What about having a silent investor in capital-intensive partnerships, such as those that purchase real estate and don't need too much management? This goal can be achieved without making the investor a partner. Structure the investor's contribution as an interest in a limited partnership, specifically defining the investing partner's role and return, which can include a share of the profits. Or treat the investment as a loan. But don't give an ownership share of your business to someone who won't work in it.

Of course, how you define major and minor will depend on the personalities of the partners and the type of business. Some partners do it by adopting money as a yardstick to define the authority of each individual partner (for example, "all decisions involving the expenditure or potential expenditure of more than $5,000 shall be discussed and voted on by all partners"). Others handle it in some other way (for example, "a decision as to what jobs to bid on, the design specifications, and the amount of the bid shall be unanimously agreed to by all partners").

Borrowing Money

It is not uncommon for a partnership to borrow money, either to get started or to expand. Normally, the lender will insist on the signature of all the partners to make sure that each partner is aware of the partnership's obligation. Banks are particularly careful about this.

Some lenders, however, won't be so fussy. The question then arises whether one partner has the power to borrow money and obligate the partnership to pay it back without the express approval of the other partners. This is something that should be covered in your partnership agreement. We recommend that you adopt a partnership agreement that requires all partners to approve all loans, unless there are special circumstances in your business that compel a different approach. It's simpler and less risky that way.

There's another potential problem here that you should be aware of. No matter what the partnership agreement states, partners in what have traditionally been called "trading partnerships" have the apparent authority to borrow money or execute loans on behalf of the partnership. Apparent authority means that outsiders can lend money to the partnership on the say-so of one partner, unless they actually know that other partners must approve the loan.

Trading partnerships are, as the name states, those directly involved in trade, like merchants selling a product. Examples of nontrading partnerships include service businesses like law firms, theaters, banks, real estate enterprises, or farms. Partners in nontrading partnerships traditionally don't have the apparent authority to borrow money on behalf of the partnership. This distinction between trading and nontrading partnerships sounds clear, but deciding which label fits a particular business is often quite difficult. Indeed, one commentator has stated that the distinction between trading and nontrading partnerships has haunted partnership law for generations. The UPA doesn't make this distinction; however, it doesn't outlaw it either, so the courts in many states still adhere to it.

CAUTION

Be especially careful if you run a retail business. In a partnership running a retail business, there is an additional danger if you have an unreliable partner. Without actual authorization by you, this partner can borrow money and leave you and the other partners stuck for the loan. This is just one more reason to choose your partners carefully.

Liability of the Partnership to the Public

Conventional legal rules of responsibility are applicable to partnerships. For example, partners must perform any services provided to the public competently, or the partnership can be liable for negligence. Competently means a partner must use the level of professional skill, care, and diligence generally applicable in the profession or trade. This standard usually applies to all partnership enterprises whether they're set up to fix teeth, trains, or toilets, or to sell soap, soup, or sawdust. So, if one partner (or an employee of the partnership) in a pest control business does a lousy home inspection and doesn't find the termites in the basement, the partnership is liable for any loss that results from that negligence.

The partnership is also liable for "any wrongful act or omission of any partner acting in the ordinary course of business of the partnership where loss or injury is caused to any person." (UPA Section 13.) This means that if a partner negligently injures a pedestrian while driving a car on partnership business, the entire partnership is liable for the pedestrian's damages. Similarly, the partnership is generally liable for intentionally wrongful acts—deceit, assault, trespass—committed by a partner during the course of partnership business.

The conventional way to protect against most business risks is to buy liability insurance. Obtaining insurance often requires you to pay a relatively high cost for protection against occurrences that are rather unlikely. However, insurance protection against traditional sorts of negligence lawsuits—for example, if someone slips and falls in your store and sues you—is obviously sensible, especially in situations where insurance is relatively affordable. Whether you want insurance against other risks, such as professional incompetence or intentional injuries, is often a more difficult choice and depends to a large degree on who you are and what you're doing. For example, legal and medical malpractice insurance has become so costly that some lawyers and doctors no longer purchase it, but choose to accept the risk that if they're sued for malpractice, they'll have to pay legal defense costs themselves—and, if they lose the case, they'll have to pay the judgment from their own assets. While this approach may make sense for website designers and copyright specialists (who are rarely sued), it might be too risky for brain surgeons and trial lawyers (whose work involves serious risks). If you are in a fairly high-risk occupation and can't get or afford insurance, you may wish to incorporate or form an LLC to take advantage of limited personal liability.

Partnership No-Nos

A partner has considerable authority to bind the partnership in the ordinary or normal course of the partnership's business. Does this mean that one partner can bind the others to anything? No. There are a number of things the Uniform Partnership Act says that a partner can't do. Members of the outside world are presumed to know a partner can't do these things "in the ordinary course of business." Here is a list of the actions a partner cannot take without partnership approval, unless the agreement specifically provides otherwise:

- convey one's interest in any partnership property ("convey" is legalese for any type of transfer, whether by sale, gift, or exchange)
- mortgage or otherwise subject partnership property to a lien to cover one's personal debts or borrowing
- attempt to dispose of specific partnership property (rather than one's own interest in the partnership) through one's will after death
- assign partnership property in trust for creditors or on the assignee's promise to pay the debts of the partnership
- dispose of the "goodwill" of the business
- commit any act that would make it impossible to carry on the ordinary business of the partnership, or
- agree to a judgment for the other side in a lawsuit against the partnership.

We do not think that any of these acts should be permitted in a partnership agreement. However, if you disagree and want a single partner to be able to mortgage property or take any of the other steps listed above, you'll have to state this expressly in your partnership agreement when defining partners' powers.

TIP

Do your homework before you buy business insurance. Deciding whether or not you need insurance by asking an insurance agent for a recommendation is a little like leaving it up to a car dealer to add on all the optional equipment he or she sees fit. A better approach is to talk to people in businesses like yours to see how they've solved the liability insurance dilemma. Once you decide on the insurance you want, shop around—rates will vary considerably.

Apparent Members of a Partnership

Here's another, and more remote, area of possible partnership danger—the possibility that you might be held liable as a member of a partnership to which you don't legally belong. This liability arises if it reasonably appears to a member of the public that you're a member of the partnership, and that person takes action based on the belief that a partnership exists.

For instance, suppose you and two acquaintances investigate forming a partnership, and even have partnership stationery printed, with all three names on it. Then you decide, for whatever reasons, to back out. Later, someone who isn't paid by the partnership for work sues you for his bill, claiming, on the basis of the letterhead and statements made by the continuing partners, that he believed you were involved and relied on this in dealing with the partnership. Is this enough to prevail against you? Maybe and maybe not; it can ultimately depend on what a jury decides, based on all the facts of the situation. Certainly, your name on a letterhead can be enough to cause someone to sue you. Who needs that worry? The point is simple—if you discuss a partnership that you don't actually join, be sure that there's no chance of the public mistaking you for a member of the partnership. If stationery or cards have been printed, destroy them. If third parties have been informed about the partnership, write to each to inform them of the true state of affairs.

Legal Rights of Partners Against a Partnership

It's at least theoretically possible that—despite your good intentions—you and your partners will end up having a spat. If you can't resolve your problems, you should know that partners do have some formal legal rights vis-à-vis their partnership. These include the right to an accounting of the partnership assets: that is, an examination of the books by an outside accountant. Periodic accountings are often provided for in partnership agreements. They are generally paid for by the partnership itself. If an accounting is made as part of a lawsuit, however, the court can apportion the cost in a way it decides is fair.

Although we hope it never happens to you, there are several types of lawsuits a partner can file against the partnership. A partner can bring a legal action for:

- dissolution—that is, to dissolve the partnership
- an injunction prohibiting the partnership from taking certain actions and appointing a receiver to handle partnership actions, and
- ordinary breach of contract.

Name and Purpose of the Partnership

A partnership business must have a name—an identity by which it presents itself to the public and the IRS. Some partnerships, such as law or accounting firms, simply choose the last names of some or all partners. Many partnerships choose two names—their own last names for their partnership, and a separate business name (called a fictitious business name) that, hopefully, will enhance their business. You can choose any name you want for your partnership or your business—except you can't pick one that's identical or very similar to one already in use. If you create a fictitious business name you must comply with the applicable state laws governing such names. These aren't generally onerous.

The partnership agreement also normally contains a short statement of the purpose of the business, such as:

- "The purpose of the Milliflower partnership is to engage in retail flower sales and any related commercial activity."
- "The purpose of the A-G partnership is to purchase, renovate, and sell residential real estate."

Generally, it's best for partners to broadly state the purpose of the partnership. There's no sensible reason to unduly narrow your scope.

You can also state the date the partnership will start and, if appropriate, when it will end. Most partnership agreements don't specify a termination date. The duration of a partnership is generally open-ended and will last as long as the partners want.

When you and your prospective partners sit down and prepare your statement of the purpose of the business, you should also take this occasion to discuss—or review—each partner's personal goals for the business. What are each partner's dreams, hopes, and fears? Surely, you'll have already voiced these concerns, but a focused summation is a good idea. Generally, we don't think you need to write your thoughts or conclusions down (no transcript is required), though there's certainly no prohibition against doing so. If you do, one good approach is to have a section in your agreement that covers each partner's sense of the goals of the business and his or her hopes for it, while making it clear this isn't intended as a binding legal provision but is offered in the spirit of making a written record of shared intentions.

Financial Considerations

Whatever your feelings about money, we've learned that a healthy, sensible respect for it is essential for a partnership business to work. Conflicts over money can destroy a partnership with astounding speed, so it's essential that all prospective partners reach an honest understanding of how you'll handle money matters and include that in your partnership agreement.

Initial Contributions to the Partnership

Your partnership will need some assets to commence business. The initial contributions, obviously, are made by you and your partners. In the simplest situation, each partner contributes cash only. Often partners contribute equal amounts, but this isn't required. In any case, if all partners are contributing cash, you should create a specific clause in your agreement that states how much money each partner will contribute.

It's also common for partners to contribute property as well as (or instead of) cash. Property contributions can range from the simple to the highly complex. In simple situations, the major matters to be covered in the partnership agreement are the value the partnership puts on the property contributed and the conditions, if any, placed on its transfer to the partnership.

Partners may also contribute their personal services. This is often a specific skill rather than simply working on partnership business. For example, three partners decide that a fourth partner will receive an owner's interest (not just wages) in a business in exchange for donating needed bookkeeping and administrative skills. However, contributing services can have adverse tax consequences for the contributing partner if it's not handled properly.

A partner can sell, lend, lease, or rent property to the partnership, too. Lending property to a partnership can be particularly appropriate if one partner possesses an item that the partnership wants to use (for example, a valuable set of antique restaurant furniture), but the partner doesn't wish to give it to the partnership, and it's too expensive for the partnership to buy.

Profits, Losses, and Draws

If your partnership agreement doesn't state how profits and losses are to be divided, the UPA provides that all partners share both equally, even if they contributed unequal amounts of cash, property, or labor to the partnership. If the partnership agreement defines how profits are to be distributed but doesn't mention losses, the UPA provides that each partner must contribute toward the losses according to his or her share of profits. (UPA Section 18(a).) However, even if profits and losses are to be shared equally, you should state this expressly in your partnership agreement, rather than rely on the UPA. This will prevent the possibility of later disagreement over what your understanding was.

Many partnerships choose to divide profits and losses unequally. This can be done for all sorts of reasons, such as when one partner contributes more work or more money to the partnership. There's no one formula for distributing profits or losses, no simple rule to tell you when it's sensible to give one or more partners a larger or smaller share. Once again, it's your business and you can divide the profits and losses any way you all agree is fair. What's crucial is that you all discuss what you want and then come to an agreement.

Sometimes partners decide that one or more partners will receive what's called a draw. The term "draw" means a periodic payment against future partnership profits. Rather than wait until the end of the taxable year to divide up profits, each partner takes a draw each month, or whatever period you've agreed on. If one partner doesn't have a financial reserve and needs money to live on each month, the partnership may decide that only that partner will receive a draw. This policy creates the risk that those who don't receive draws will resent payments to a partner who gets them.

SEE A LAWYER

Check with a lawyer if you want to allow partnership salaries.
The IRS has strict and rather confusing rules on whether a member of a partnership can also be an employee of that partnership. (Treasury Decision 9766, 81 FR 26693-26695; IRS Rev Rul. 69-184.) Partners can, of course, take draws from partnership funds, as well as profits from the partnership business. But if for some reason you want to allow a partner to also be an employee, check with an experienced partnership lawyer or accountant to see if the IRS will allow it.

Owning Property

Property owned by a partnership is held in the partnership name. (UPA Section 25.) Partners, however, are free to decide whether property used by the business will be partnership property or will be owned by an individual partner and merely used by the partnership (that is, rented, leased, or loaned and used free). Unless the partners expressly agree to the contrary, property acquired with partnership funds is partnership property.

> EXAMPLE: Eduardo and Louise are partners in a local parcel delivery business. Eduardo has two trucks of his own, which they occasionally use in the business. Eduardo enters into a simple written agreement with the partnership, which states that the partnership will compensate Eduardo a certain amount per mile for use of the trucks. In this situation, there's no implication that the trucks belong to the partnership. But if Eduardo's trucks wear out and the partnership buys a truck with partnership assets, this new truck is clearly a partnership asset, even if Eduardo uses it occasionally for personal errands.

Property held in the partnership name can only be sold and transferred by the partnership itself. There are advantages to this. Aside from protection against unethical partners, partnership property isn't subject to attachment or execution to satisfy a creditor's individual claim against one partner.

If the partnership agreement or the partners haven't defined which items are partnership property, here are the four questions courts usually ask in determining whether property belongs to the partnership:

- What was the source of funds used to buy it?
- Was it purchased in the partnership name?
- Was it used in the partnership business?
- Was it reflected on the books as a partnership asset?

Taxes

We discuss partnership taxation, especially as it concerns a beginning partnership, in Chapter 8. There are, however, a few tax matters you should know about up front.

- The partnership doesn't pay taxes itself, but it must file an "informational" partnership tax return (IRS Form 1065).
- Partners pay taxes on all net profits, whether actually distributed to the partners or not.
- Partnerships must use the accrual method of accounting "whenever inventories of goods are maintained." (The accrual method of accounting means debits and credits are counted when accrued, not when money is actually received or paid. For example, if a business sells flowers and bills for its services, the sale is counted when it is invoiced, not when the customer actually pays.)
- Partnerships or partners are allowed to deduct money spent organizing or promoting a partnership only over a period of years (rather than in the partnership's first tax year).
- Contributions of property or services to a partnership can raise complex tax problems.

The tax implications of contributions to a partnership, especially property contributions, can become quite complicated. For example, if one partner wants to contribute property bought long ago at a low price—property that is now worth far more—does that partner have to pay taxes on this gain when the partnership gets ownership of the property? Is this transfer a taxable event? The answer is generally no. However, if the transferred property is subject to a mortgage, the tax situation becomes murkier, and the contributing partner may be assessed a taxable gain.

(!) CAUTION

Existing businesses that bring in a partner might have more complications. Depending on your state, problems could arise if a merchant decides to take in a partner and the merchant's inventory will be transferred to the partnership. Some states have "bulk sales" laws governing the transfer of a business owner's inventory to a new owner. Many states have repealed their Bulk Sales laws, and replaced them as part of the Uniform Commercial Code (UCC). However, the details of UCC bulk sales provisions can vary from state to state. Also, a number of states, including California, have retained their bulk sales laws. If you plan to take in a new partner or partners who will transfer business inventory to the partnership, check with a knowledgeable lawyer about how your state's laws can affect this transfer of business inventory.

Expanding Your Business

We urge you to discuss how you and your partners will handle it if your business takes off and prospers greatly. How much income is sufficient before each of you will feel satisfied? Will any of you want to kick back and develop other interests, or will you all redouble your efforts to become more prosperous? Think about how each of you will feel hiring employees, hiring more employees, moving to a new store or office, adding a second facility, expanding into a related business, buying additional machinery, financing a larger staff or inventory, taking over an ongoing operation, and so on. If partners feel very differently about many of these issues, it's an indication that perhaps they should rethink the idea of going into business together.

While you should talk about these matters, we don't feel it's normally advisable to put specific provisions in your original partnership agreement that provide an expansion game plan, with one important exception: adding partners. The reason that there's not much point in incorporating details of how you'll handle future growth in your original agreement is that generally it's quite futile to try to predict your business future.

As a practical matter, any specifics regarding expansion that you put in your agreement now aren't likely to be of any use in legally binding a partner. If, a couple of years down the road, your partner doesn't like the way the business is expanding, all the legal clauses in the world aren't likely to make him or her more cooperative. Courts won't issue orders compelling a partner to live up to a clause agreeing to work productively for an expanded business; how could the court enforce it? Remember, the essence of partnership is voluntary cooperation. If you and your partners begin to fundamentally disagree about the direction your partnership business should take, it's time to go your separate ways. A well-drafted partnership agreement can help you negotiate the split, but it can't make you continue to work together productively.

Operational and Management Responsibilities

It's desirable, and usually essential, that each partner be actively involved in managing and operating the partnership business. Aside from the practical, commonsense reasons for this, it's generally desirable for income tax purposes.

When preparing your agreement, you should be sure everyone feels comfortable with how work and responsibilities have been divided up. As for the specific clauses in your agreement, there's no ironclad rule about how you should describe each partner's work responsibilities. If there are only two or three partners, and they will all be involved in all phases of the business, a simple statement to that effect will usually suffice. On the other hand, if your business will involve more separation of management roles, or if, whatever the work duties involved, you feel more comfortable with precision on this subject, feel free to define the details of management responsibilities in your agreement.

If you decide to be specific about management responsibilities, here are some key issues you will probably want to cover:
- skills to be contributed by each partner
- hours worked

- work duties of each partner (the specific tasks and functions of the business for which each partner has primary responsibility), and
- management roles (aspects of the business that each partner has primary responsibility to control and direct, either by his or her own efforts or by supervising employees).

If you think it's advisable, you can be even more specific, covering matters like expense account rules and check-signing procedures.

Withdrawal of a Partner, Buyouts, and Ending a Partnership

It's absolutely essential that you adopt rules for what happens if a partner leaves—whether by withdrawal, death or illness, or expulsion. How much notice of withdrawal must a departing partner give? Can that partner sell his or her interest? To whom? Do the remaining partners have the right to buy out the departing partner? How is the buyout price determined? What is the payment schedule? What happens if there are only two partners and one leaves? Or suppose there are an equal number of partners divided into two opposing groups, both of which want to continue the business?

Rules for a Partner's Departure

When you're preparing your agreement, you must focus on issues raised by the departure of a partner. You need to specify in your partnership agreement how the value of a departing partner's interest is determined. Also, do the remaining partners have the right (or option) to buy a departing partner's interest? Usually, it's a good idea to provide for this. We'll get into this in depth in Chapter 5.

Once you decide on how to value a partnership share, there's the question of payment. Naturally, a departing partner usually prefers to receive full payment in cash, immediately. However, the remaining partners may face the destruction of the business unless payments can be made over time. A prior agreement on how payments are to be made eliminates these conflicts.

RESOURCE

More information on buyout agreements. While Chapter 5 discusses buyouts in some detail, see *Business Buyout Agreements*, by Anthony Mancuso and Bethany Laurence (Nolo), for even more in-depth information on this topic.

Ending a Partnership

The legal term for the ending of a partnership is "dissolution." When a partnership ends, the partnership business ends too. The partners can't undertake new partnership business. They must pay all the bills and distribute any remaining assets to the soon-to-be ex-partners. (This is discussed in Chapter 5.)

By definition, a partnership ends if there were only two partners, and one leaves. In any larger partnership, the departure of one partner usually doesn't result in a termination of the business; the other partners carry it on.

Disputes

The last major area to cover in your agreement is what happens if the partners have a dispute they can't resolve. Of course, you should do all you can to avoid having to resolve disputes in a formal way. However, despite your best efforts, it's possible that a dispute will arise that the partners can't resolve between themselves. For this reason, we urge you to include a mediation/arbitration clause in your partnership agreement. (See Chapter 6.)

No clause can prevent a partner from leaving a partnership. Not even a court would order a person to remain active in a partnership against that person's wishes. But with mediation/arbitration, at least the issues between the partners will be settled reasonably and promptly, without a court fight.

Mediation

Mediation is a process in which an outside party—the mediator—attempts to help people resolve a dispute by reaching a mutually satisfactory compromise or resolution. A mediator has no power to impose a decision, which means there's no guarantee you'll resolve the matter unless you and your partners can find some common ground. However, if mediation is successful, the partners will generally have reached an agreement into which everyone's had input, and which hasn't been imposed on them by a court or an arbitrator. This can help all the partners feel good about the legitimacy and fairness of the compromise.

Arbitration

In arbitration, your dispute is submitted to an arbitrator, who has the power to make a binding decision. The arbitration process is usually fairly informal, depending on the arbitrator's personality and any arbitration rules you have agreed on. An arbitrator's decision is exceedingly difficult to challenge successfully in court, so it's almost always final.

Your partnership agreement can provide for binding arbitration by various methods, from naming a trusted friend to selecting a group of three colleagues. It can be wise to name a specific arbitrator, who all the partners respect, in the initial agreement.

Combining Arbitration With Mediation

We suggest that you include both mediation and arbitration clauses in your agreement. Any dispute is first referred to a mediator. But if the partners fail to agree, you'll next present the dispute to an arbitrator rather than go to court. For example, you could state that if mediation proved unsuccessful after a certain period of time, arbitration would follow.

Short-Form Partnership Agreements

For some people, there can be a time gap between starting a partnership, perhaps with a handshake, and the final signing of a comprehensive partnership agreement. For those who may need a stopgap device that does little more than establish the fact that you have created a partnership, we include a short-term partnership agreement with this book (see Appendix B and C). This short-form agreement is no substitute for the complete agreement you will want to create for your partnership and should only be used if you need time to work out the details of your final agreement.

Will You Need a Lawyer or an Accountant?

Many people successfully create their partnership agreement on their own, particularly with the help of resources like this book. Whether or not you'll want to consult with a lawyer will depend on several factors including:

- How complicated is your business?
- How much time and effort have you expended on your agreement?
- How complicated is that agreement?
- How much money are partners investing?

- How complex are your tax issues, particularly regarding contributions of property or services?
- Does your partnership involve a high-tech service or product and issues regarding intellectual property rights, such as patents, copyrights, or trademarks?
- Are there any issues you want to cover in your agreement that still trouble you?
- How confident do you feel that you understand partnerships and that your agreement is sound and complete?

In addition, if one or more partners, especially one who plans to make a major investment, is much less sophisticated than the others, all partners have a real interest in making sure that person gets professional advice. If you decide you want to use a lawyer, you can check Nolo's Lawyer Directory at www.nolo.com. You will find profiles of lawyers who advertise, including their areas of expertise and geographical location.

Most businesses will need the help of an accountant, at least at tax time. But particularly as you start up, don't get hooked into paying for a more complicated accounting system than you need. ●

Partnership Name, Contributions, Profits, and Management

Th
his chapter provides clauses covering basic partnership issues (Clauses 1 through 6 of the partnership agreement included in this book). Be prepared to talk issues over and keep notes, because you'll be starting to pin down what will actually be in your final agreement.

Completing Sample Clauses

In this chapter and Chapters 4, 5, 6, and 7, we discuss the clauses that are in the Partnership Agreement included with this book. As you proceed through these chapters, hash out what you want to do with each subject covered. Once you decide which clause, or clauses, you want to include in your agreement, fill in the blank lines with the appropriate information. You can use the check box to keep track of which clauses you want to include in your final agreement and you may also want to keep notes about what you want in your clauses.

Name, Term, and Purpose

Your partnership, your business, and your product (if you have one) need names. You also need to state the term of the partnership—how long it will last—and its basic business purpose.

Choosing Partnership, Business, or Product Names

You will give your partnership a name in the partnership agreement (see Clause 1). Your business or product also will have a name, which may or may not be the same as the partnership name. As for the titles the partners take for themselves, you can call yourselves partners, managing partners, or anything you want.

The name of the partnership is often the last names of the partners. For example, "The partnership shall be called Smith, Weiss and Fong." However, this isn't mandatory. If the business will use a fictitious name (a name other than the names of its partners), the partners may decide to give the partnership the same name, so the enterprise has only one name.

There is one legal restriction on the name of a partnership: A partnership cannot legally hold itself out to be a corporation. This means that you can't use the words "Inc.," "Ltd.," "Corporation," "Incorporated" (or in some states, "Company" or "Co."), or "Foundation" after your name. However, terms that don't directly imply that you're incorporated, such as "Associates," "Affiliates," "Group," and "Organization," are normally okay. Check with your secretary of state's office (find yours at the website of the National Association of Secretaries of State at www.nass.org) or take a look at your state's UPA or Revised UPA to determine which terms you may (or may not) use in your partnership's name.

If you do choose to use a fictitious business (or partnership) name, you could run into serious problems if you choose a name another business is already using. So, let's take a closer look at how you can sensibly choose a name for your business.

The Importance of Your Business or Product Name

Your business or product name may turn out to be one of your most important business assets, as it can come to represent the goodwill of your business. We don't mean this just in an accounting or tax sense. The people and institutions you do business with will identify you mostly by your business name or associate certain characteristics with the name of your product. For this reason, as well as a number of practical reasons (such as not wanting to print new stationery or checks, change promotional literature, create new logos, and so on,) you will want to select a name you'll be happy with for a long time.

If your business has a product, you should think about whether you will market the product nationally, or in other states. If so, you should check on the legal availability of the name you choose for that product. And if your business offers a service, consider whether you might ever sell that service to a broad market. Clearly, you don't want to begin marketing your product or service nationally and then learn, perhaps via a lawsuit, that some business in another state or area already has a trademark on the name you are using.

Checking on the Legal Availability of a Name

Whatever name you decide to use for your partnership, product, or both (even your own names), check to be sure another business isn't already using that name, or one confusingly similar. Business names often are legally protected trademarks, or service marks. This means that a business with a prior claim to a name identical or similar to yours can sue to enjoin (stop) you from using the name or can force you to change it. A court may even award money damages to the name's rightful owner for any sales or goodwill it loses due to your use of the name.

Checking on the legal availability of a name can take some work. Perhaps the easiest thing to do is to go to the U.S. Patent and Trademark Office's website, www.uspto.gov. From there, click on "searching trademarks" under the Trademarks section. This will take you to the USPTO's registered trademark database ("TESS"), which you can search for free. In addition, from the main USPTO website, you can download forms and get answers to frequently asked questions. You can also conduct a name search by locating a Patent and Trademark Resource Center (PTRC). All states have at least one of these centers. To locate them, you can ask a local research librarian, or search "PTRC" at www.uspto.gov.

In addition to choosing your business name, it's wise to also choose an available Internet domain name, the address your customers use to reach your website, such as Nolo.com. Start by doing an online search of the names you're considering, and check one of the many inexpensive domain name registrars, such as www.namecheap.com.

RESOURCE

Want to know more about trademarks? You can obtain much more information on naming your business or product and conducting name searches from *Trademark: Legal Care for Your Business & Product Name,* by Stephen Fishman (Nolo). It covers just about everything you might need to know about trademark law. In addition to educating you about trademark law, the book should aid you in choosing a strong marketing name, and, if the circumstances warrant, help you register your business or product name as a trademark with state and federal trademark agencies.

One way to create a name that doesn't conflict with another business's trademark can be to geographically limit your name, adding a particular limitation, such as "of Georgia," "in Northern Wyoming," or "in downtown Los Angeles." So, if you call yourself Southern Oregon Lumber, and you are the only one, you should be okay. But even here, it pays to check. If there is an Oregon Lumber Co., and they operate in Southern Oregon, they might object that your name is confusingly similar. Also, this approach works best only if you're sure your business will not offer goods or services outside of your local geographic area.

Protecting Your Name

Once you've decided on a fictitious product or business name that you have concluded is available for you to use, you may want to register it either with your secretary of state or with the U.S. Patent and Trademark Office as a trademark or service mark.

Federal registration costs $225 to $400 if you are filing electronically and up to $600 if you are filing a paper application. To register, one of the following must be true:

1. You have actually used the name in interstate commerce (that is, in two or more states) in connection with the marketing of goods or services.

2. You intend to use the name in interstate commerce in connection with the marketing of goods or services.

If you specify the second reason in your trademark application, you must file an affidavit (sworn statement) within six months stating that the name has been placed in actual use. This costs an additional $100. This allows you to reserve ownership of a trademark before actually using it.

You might wonder if there are any benefits to registering your business or product name as a trademark. First, if you register your business or product name as a trademark or service mark, it will be placed on the Principal Register of all registered trademarks maintained by the USPTO. This means that other would-be users are on notice that you own the mark, and that you have the exclusive right to use the mark nationwide. And, once it's registered, the law presumes that you are the legal owner of the trademark, which means you won't have to prove ownership if you get into a dispute with another business over its use. So while it may seem a bit expensive, if you're going to market your services or products nationally, it might be worthwhile.

Filing a Fictitious Name Statement

If you use any or all of the partners' last names for your business, you do not have to register the business name with any government agency (but as mentioned, it may be a good idea to file trademark registrations). If you use a fictitious business name, state law or local ordinances normally require you to register that name. This is neither a complicated nor particularly expensive procedure. Registering a fictitious business name at the state or county level typically involves filing a single statement, often referred to as a dba or d/b/a (doing business as), and in some states, publishing a series of brief notices in a local newspaper. Contact your secretary of state, city or county clerk, or tax and license officer for more information.

In unusual circumstances, a partnership using a fictitious name may not have to file a fictitious name statement. If the partnership will not conduct business or earn income, no statement is required. What type of partnership, you may ask, doesn't intend to make money? They are rare, but occasionally people create a partnership for an informal club. For instance, a group of investors who wish to share advice may want to create a partnership agreement to define how they'll work together, but the partnership itself will not buy or sell stocks. If the partnership is given a fictitious name in this type of agreement, no fictitious name statement is necessary.

TIP
Check the Internet for state and local government information and forms. To find state and local government information on the Internet, check out www.statelocalgov.net, which provides links to state, county, and city websites. Other useful websites for listings of relevant state government agencies include the Small Business Administration (www.sba.gov) and the IRS (ww.irs.gov).

Who Keeps the Name If the Partnership Splits Up?

Who gets the right to continue to use the business name, product name, or a website domain name if the partners split up? An obvious example of a business with a desirable name is a successful rock band, but don't ignore this concern because your business is more mundane. The name of a successful bakery, restaurant, or dry cleaner can also have real value. It's best to assume your business name will have value in the marketplace and to define in your partnership agreement who will retain rights to the name if a partner leaves or the partnership ends. (See Chapter 5.)

CAUTION

Think about potential ownership issues before you put your name on a partnership. Putting your own name on a business can cause problems if you sell out or leave and the business continues. You may have sold the right to use your own name for that type of business. If you decide to use your name for the name of your partnership, make sure you and your partners agree on who will get the right to use the name when and if the partnership ends.

Choosing Your Partnership and Business Names

Following is a clause you can complete to state your partnership and business names.

NAME

☐ The name of the partnership shall be _____

_____.

☐ The name of the partnership business shall be

_____.

Term of the Partnership

Many partnership agreements do not state how long the partnership will last or provide a termination date. Legally, this means the partnership lasts indefinitely—usually until one partner departs or dies, or the partners agree to dissolve the partnership. Even so, it is best to clearly state the circumstances under which the partnership will terminate (see Clause 2 of the agreement). You can also, of course, decide that the partnership will end on a certain date.

Here's a basic open-ended term clause:

Lasts Until Dissolved on Death of Partner

☐ The partnership shall last until it is dissolved by all the partners, or a partner leaves, for any reason, including death.

Whether you wish to state a specific date when the partnership will end or that it will last until ended by a partner's death or departure, be sure your duration clause is coordinated with your buyout clause. (See Chapter 5.) Here's a more specific clause that requires you to cross-reference your buyout clause.

Lasts Until Dissolved or Partner Withdraws

☐ The partnership shall last until it is dissolved by all the partners or until a partner withdraws, retires, dies, or otherwise leaves the partnership, under Sections _____ and _____ of this Agreement.

Sometimes partners decide they don't want an open-ended agreement. This is particularly true in joint ventures (partnerships for a specific limited purpose or project). Here are some sample clauses to limit the term of a partnership.

Lasts for Set Term of Years

☐ The partnership shall commence as of the date of this Agreement and shall continue for a period of _____ years, at which time it shall be dissolved and its affairs wound up.

Lasts Until Set Event

☐ The partnership shall continue until [*specify an event, such as "the sale of 126 Venture Street, Albany, New York"*], at which time it shall be dissolved and its affairs wound up.

Purpose of the Partnership

Your partnership agreement should contain a short statement of the basic purpose of the business (see Clause 3). Generally, it's wise to state the purpose broadly, to allow for possible expansion of the business.

EXAMPLE: Three partners plan to start a consulting business to provide specialized advice on the employment problems of county governments in Colorado. At first, they decide to simply say that in their purpose clause. Then they ask themselves what happens if the business does well. Perhaps the next step would be to do consulting for governmental entities generally or for a mix of governmental and private clients in fields other than employment and outside of Colorado. After considerable discussion, they decide it makes sense to define the business purpose as consulting in the public and private sectors, and leave out limiting words like "employment," "county governments," and "Colorado."

Another way to deal with the same problem would be to include both definitions as to the scope of the business. That is to say, you might draft something like this:

The original purpose of our partnership business is to provide high-quality consulting services to county governments in the State of Colorado concerning employee relations. However, it is also contemplated that in the future, general consulting services may be offered to governmental and private business units at all levels within and without Colorado.

Some partnerships don't want a broad purpose clause. For instance, if you're engaged in a limited enterprise, such as a joint venture, it's likely you will want to limit that business by purpose as well as by time. If a partner will also work in a closely related business, you'll need to exclude that type of work from your "purpose" to prevent possible conflict of interest problems later. (See "Management Responsibilities," below, for specific clauses related to partners' possible conflicts of interest.)

Here's a basic form for your purpose clause:

Statement of the Partnership's Purpose

☐ The purpose of the partnership is: _____

_____

_____.

Statements of Partners' Goals

The partners may decide to include a short written statement of each partner's goals and hopes for the partnership. One way to do this is to include a short recital in the agreement. A recital normally has no legal effect; its purpose is simply to state, in writing, facts that the partners want to stress.

Here's a basic clause you can use or adapt to state partners' goals, if you decide you want that.

Statement of Partners' Goals

☐ The specific purposes of the partnership are set out above. In addition, the goals and dreams of each partner are set out below. The partners understand that this clause is not legally binding, but include it in the Partnership Agreement as a record of their hopes and intentions:

_____.

Contributions

One of the first things you and your partners will need to decide is how much cash, property, or services each partner will contribute to the partnership, as well as what happens if the partnership eventually needs more money. That's the focus of Clause 4 of the partnership agreement.

If each partner contributes an equal amount, each will (presumably) be an equal owner of the business. But what if the partners make unequal contributions? Then you need to decide how you want ownership to work. You can all still be equal owners as far as equity in the business goes, but later on, when it comes to division of profits, you can provide for unequal division. Or you can provide for this in unequal ownership.

Capital Account

You will encounter the term "capital account" often in your partnership business. Simply stated, a partner's capital account is the dollar value of his or her ownership interest in the business, the partner's total equity in the business. A partner's capital account will be adjusted over the life of the partnership to reflect profits allocated to that partner, distributions made, and each partner's share of losses and liabilities. It's important for partners to keep good records so that when the partnership is dissolved or a partner sells his or her interest, the partner pays the correct amount of income taxes on any gain in the value of that interest.

EXAMPLE: Merv and Hayden start a business booking comedians into clubs and college campus venues. Each contributes $40,000 cash, so each partner's capital account starts out at $40,000. Now suppose the business loses a net $10,000 the first year, or $5,000 a partner. Each partner's capital account will now be $35,000.

Determining the value of a partner's capital account can be far more complex if, for instance, the partnership owns appreciated property or inventory. Once a business is underway, it often requires an accountant experienced with partnership issues to determine the current value of a capital account.

Regarding contributions, we've already stressed that there's a real potential for conflict if there's a significant disparity between work and money contributed by different partners. The person who contributes the most of either may come to resent the others, especially if the business gets off to a slow start. At the very least, you need to recognize that unequal contributions can cause problems in the partnership, and talk out what's mutually comfortable—or at least acceptable—before you go into business together.

> **SEE AN EXPERT**
>
> **Get legal help if you're considering paying a partner a salary.** If one partner will work much more than the other, it's permissible, under tax laws, to pay that partner a salary. Compensation to a working partner is a deductible business expense, as long as the salary is reasonable compared to what's generally paid for similar work in the industry. In other words, the salary cannot be a disguised distribution of profits. However, this can create complicated taxes for both the partnership and the partner who receives the salary, so if you're interested in doing this, get some help from a knowledgeable tax attorney or accountant experienced with partnership issues. In addition, keep in mind that this salary won't be tied to whether the partnership actually makes a profit. For this reason, you should carefully consider whether you want to commit the partnership to paying this money.

Cash Contributions

Frequently, each partner contributes cash to a new business. A key decision here is whether each partner contributes an equal amount. If this is possible, we think it's desirable; otherwise, the partners who contribute the most cash may want more than an equal say in management decisions, which can lead to problems down the road.

But sometimes, partners simply can't afford to contribute the same amount of cash. There are many ways to handle the problems inherent in this disparity. One is to have what would otherwise be the excess cash contributed by one partner converted to a loan; in other words, all partners make equal contributions, and one partner also lends money to the business.

> EXAMPLE: Naomi and Toni open a modern dance studio. They both contribute $40,000, and Naomi lends the business an additional $30,000 at 5% annual interest, to be repaid over three years.

SEE AN EXPERT

See a lawyer before allowing a partner to lend money to a partner or the partnership. Having a partner lend money to partners or the partnership is unusual for most beginning businesses. A complicated financial transaction like that is far beyond what most partners need or want. If you are seriously considering having a partner lend money to your business or to the partners individually, it's wise to see a lawyer regarding that transaction.

Another solution is to have the partners who contribute less cash work more, often at a set rate, to equalize contributions.

Equal Cash Contribution

☐ The initial capital of the partnership shall be a total of $_____.
Each partner shall contribute an equal share amounting to $_____,
no later than _____, 20___. Each partner shall own an equal share
of the business.

Unequal Cash Contribution

☐ The initial capital of the partnership shall consist of cash to be
contributed by the partners in the following amounts:

Name	Amount
_____	$_____
_____	$_____
_____	$_____
_____	$_____

Each partner's contribution shall be paid in full by

_____, 20_____.

Each partner's ownership share of the business shall be:

Name   Share

_____

_____

_____

Equal Cash Contributions, With a Partner Lending Additional Cash

☐ The initial capital of the partnership shall be a total of $_____.

Each partner shall contribute an equal share amounting to $_____,

no later than _____, 20___. In addition, ____[name]_____

shall lend the partnership $_____ by _____, 20____.

The partnership shall pay ____ percent interest on the loan.

Unequal Cash Contributions, to Be Equalized By One Partner's Extra Work in the Business

☐ The initial capital of the partnership shall consist of cash to be

contributed by the partners in the following amounts:

Name   Amount

_____ $_____

_____ $_____

_____ $_____

_____ $_____

Each partner's contribution shall be paid in full by _____, 20___.

In addition, to equalize the contributions, ____[name]_____ shall

contribute an extra _____ hours of work __[per day or week, etc.]__ valued

at $_____ until the amount contributed by all partners is equal.

Contributions are one area of partnership agreements that can get very complex. Clauses for some of the more common variations are set out below.

Deferred Contributions

If a partner cannot initially contribute the desired amount of cash, the partnership could require deferred contributions—in other words, payments over time. These deferred payments can be arranged any way you decide upon, including equal monthly installments, or payments from business profits.

Monthly Installments

☐ _____ shall be a partner, but shall not make any contribution of cash or property to the initial capital of the partnership. ___[He/She]___ shall subsequently contribute to the partnership capital, and _____[his/her]_____capital account shall be credited, in the amount of $_____ per month, beginning _____, 20__, until ___[he/she]_____ has contributed the sum of $_____.

Contribution Out of Profit

☐ _____ shall be a partner, but shall not make any contribution of cash or property to the initial capital of the partnership. ____[He/She]___ shall subsequently contribute to the partnership capital, and ___[his/her]_____ capital account shall be credited _____ % of ___[his/her]__ share of the partnership profits for each fiscal year, beginning _____, 20_____, until ____[he/she]_____ has contributed the amount of $_____.

Paying Interest on Contributed Capital

Should partners receive interest payments from the business on contributed capital? Generally, the answer is no. Why pay interest to yourselves for the money you invest in your own business? If you decide no partner can receive interest for contributions, it's best to state this explicitly in your agreement, as provided in the clause below.

No Interest Paid

☐ No partner shall be entitled to receive any interest on any capital contribution.

In rare instances, partners decide they want to pay interest on capital contributions. Perhaps one partner has contributed more cash to the business than others and wants to receive interest on that contribution. In effect, this turns the contribution into a loan. Rather than pay interest, it's usually better to be direct and call it a loan. After all, why should a partner receive both an ownership interest and interest for making a contribution?

If interest is paid, many payment variations are possible. For example, you might specify that partners receive interest only in years when net profits exceed a specified percent, that only a certain partner receives interest, that interest is optional and shall be decided upon yearly by the partners, and so on.

If, despite our suggestion, you decide to pay interest on contributions, use or adapt the following clause.

Interest to Be Paid

☐ [Each partner] or [Name of individual partner] shall be entitled to interest on his or her capital contribution accruing at the rate of ____ percent per year from the date the contribution is paid. This interest shall be treated as an expense to be charged against income on the partnership books and shall be paid to the partner entitled to it ____ [specify terms, for example, "quarterly" or "only upon termination of the partnership"] ____ .

Contributions of Property

It's common for partners to contribute property as well as (or instead of) cash to a partnership. This can be real property (real estate) or personal property (everything else). Also, a partner can sell or lease personal or real property to a partnership. Obviously, property contribution scenarios can range from the simple to the exceedingly complex. In simple situations, the major matters covered in the partnership agreement are the value the partnership puts on the property contributed and the conditions, if any, placed on its transfer to the partnership.

> **CAUTION**
>
> **Be sure to check the tax aspects of contributions of property carefully, especially if the property has appreciated in value.** If a partner will contribute appreciated property, you may well need the assistance of a partnership tax expert before finalizing your agreement. We discuss these tax issues in Chapter 8.

Contributions of Real or Personal Property

Following is a sample clause that can be used, or adapted, when a partner contributes property to the partnership. Of course, this clause (or any other property contribution clause) can also be combined with a cash contribution clause, if you have one.

Specific Property Contributed

☐ _____ shall contribute property valued at $_____, consisting of *[If the property is difficult to describe, describe it in detail on a separate sheet of paper marked "Exhibit A" and add here "and more particularly described in Exhibit A, attached to this Agreement."]* by _____, 20____.

(If more than one partner contributes property, repeat this clause for each partner.)

A partner may lend specific items of property, such as tools, antiques, or vehicles, to the partnership. Often, the partnership won't pay a fee to use the property (though you can provide for that if you decide to). You also need to decide when the items are to be returned. This could be when the partnership ends, when the lending partner wants the property back, or after a set period of time, such as one year.

Here's a clause for loans of property to the partnership.

Loans of Property to the Partnership

☐ In addition to the capital contributions defined in this Agreement, some partners have or will lend to the partnership additional items of property, as specified below:

_____ shall lend ___*[item identified]*___

_____ shall lend ___*[item identified]*___

(If the property is not simple to describe, you can add "more particularly described in Exhibits A, B, and so on, attached to this Agreement.")

Each item of property lent to the partnership shall remain the separate property of the lending partner and shall be returned to that partner _*[insert whatever terms you've agreed on—for example, "upon dissolution of the partnership, or "upon demand," and so on]*___ .

Contributions of Intellectual Property

Partners may also contribute intellectual property—legal rights to a copyright, patent, trademark, or trade secret. For these unique forms of property, it's important to clearly define what that contribution means. For example, is the partner transferring all rights to the business? Or just the use of the intellectual property during the existence of the business? And who controls derivative rights, including the right to license the intellectual property to others?

Intellectual Property—Ownership Transferred to the Partnership

☐ ___[Name]___ , the owner of _____ [describe, such as "patent # _____ for [describe patented subject]" or "the copyright to [name] dated "]__ , hereby agrees to transfer all _[his/her]_ interest in this _[patent/copyright]__ to the partnership with the understanding that all _[his/her]_ interest in the _[patent/copyright]__ , including the sole right to license derivative works, shall vest in, and be owned by, the partnership and shall not be _[his/her]_ separate property. In exchange for this transfer, it is agreed that __[name]__ shall be credited with a contribution of $_____ to the partnership. No sale or assignment of, or grant of license under, the _[patent/copyright]__ shall be made without the consent of all the partners. Any monies resulting from any such sale, assignment, or grant of license shall be divided [equally among the partners] or [among the partners in accordance with the allocation of profits specified in this Agreement].

Intellectual Property—Only Use Transferred to the Partnership

☐ ___[Name]___ , the owner of _[describe, such as "patent # _____ for [describe patented subject]" or "the copyright to [name], dated"]__ hereby contributes to the partnership the nonexclusive use of that __[patent/copyright]__ , with the understanding that __[he/she]__ shall retain sole ownership of the __[patent/copyright]__ , along with the sole right to license its use to third parties, and it shall not become a partnership asset. [Name]__ further agrees that until the termination of the partnership, or until __[his/her]__ death or retirement from it, __[he/she]__ will not, without the consent of all other partners, sell, assign, or grant licenses under this __[patent/copyright]__ . Any money accruing from a sale or assignment of, or the grant of licenses under, such __[patent/copyright]__ , which are so authorized, shall be the sole property of ___[name]___ .

For the purpose of profit-sharing only, and not for participation in the distribution upon the termination and winding up of the partnership, the partnership will credit _____ *[name]* _____ with a contribution in the amount of $_____.

Contributions of Services

In some cases, one or more of the partners will receive an interest in the business in exchange for a promise to donate personal services to the business. For example, Elsa and Daphne form a partnership owned 50% by each to cater events. Each will spend equal time on food preparation and service. Elsa contributes $10,000 to get the business going. Daphne agrees to contribute unpaid labor as a bookkeeper and business manager for nine months over and above the time she spends on parties, because she doesn't have the money to match Elsa's cash contribution.

Here's a clause covering the contribution of services:

Contribution of Services

☐ ___*[Name]*_____ shall make no cash or property contribution at the commencement of the partnership. __*[Name]*__ shall donate __*["[his/her]* *full work time" or "hours per week," etc.]*__ , and energies to the partnership for a period of _____ and for those services __*[he/she]*__ shall be entitled to ___ percent ownership of the business.

Sometimes, the partners contributing cash or property want the service partner to eventually equal their cash contributions. One way to do that is to require that the service partner not receive a full share of the profits until he or she has contributed a certain amount. These situations are very individual, and there's no simple, set clause to cover it. You need to create a solution you all think is fair, then write it down, by using or adapting the following clause.

Contribution of Profits From Service Partner

☐ Should *[service-contributing partner's]* share of the profits, as defined in this Agreement, exceed *[insert whatever you've agreed upon]*, *[he/she]* shall contribute the excess to *[his/her]* capital account in the business until the total amount of *[his/her]* capital account shall *[equal the separate capital contributions made by [name] and [name]]* or *[insert specific dollar amount]*.

RELATED TOPIC

There may be adverse tax consequences for a partner who contributes services. See Chapter 8 for more information.

Failure to Make Initial Contribution

What happens if a partner simply fails to contribute the initial cash or property required by the partnership agreement? The first question here is whether you want to concern yourself with this as part of your agreement. After all, don't you trust your partners to put up what they say they will? On the other hand, if for some reason one partner proves unwilling or unable to meet this obligation, you'll probably be in better shape if you've already decided how to handle it. Does the business break up or not? Is that partner expelled from the partnership?

Here are three approaches to this issue.

Partnership Dissolves

☐ If any partner fails to pay his or her initial contribution to the partnership as required by this Agreement, the partnership shall immediately dissolve and each partner who has paid all or any portion of his or her initial contribution to the partnership's capital shall be entitled to a return of the funds and properties he or she contributed.

In the following clause, you're agreeing that if one partner doesn't make the required capital contributions, that partner is expelled from the partnership. The expelled partner's interest is then allocated pro rata to the other partners.

Partnership Continues for Partners Who Have Made Contributions, and No Additional Contribution Required

☐ If any partner fails to pay his or her contribution to the partnership's capital as required by this Agreement, the partnership shall not dissolve or terminate, but it shall continue as a partnership of only the partners who have made their initial capital contributions as required and without any partner who has failed to do so. In that case, the share in the partnership's profits and losses allocated under this Agreement to any partner who has failed to make his or her initial contribution shall be reallocated to the remaining partners in proportion to their respective shares of partnership profits and losses as specified in this Agreement.

In the next clause, you're also agreeing that a partner who fails to make a required capital contribution is expelled from the partnership. However, instead of the partnership doing without that money, you're requiring the other partners to contribute that money in proportion to their respective partnership interests.

Partnership Continues—Additional Contributions Are Required

☐ If any person fails to pay his or her initial contributions to the partnership's capital as required by this Agreement, the partnership shall not dissolve or terminate, but shall continue as a partnership of the partners who have made their initial capital contributions and without any person who shall have failed to do so, but only if the remaining partners pay the initial capital contribution that was to have been made by the noncontributing partner or partners. The partnership shall promptly give written notice of this failure to all partners who have made their initial capital contributions. The notice shall specify the amount not paid. Within _____ days after the notice is given, the remaining partners shall pay the amount of the defaulted contribution in proportion to the respective amount they are required to pay to the partnership's capital under this Agreement. That share of the profits of the partnership belonging to noncontributing partners shall then be reallocated to the remaining partners in proportion to their respective shares of partnership profits and losses under this Agreement.

Finally, there's the often more troubling question of service contributions. These can be more difficult because they're made over time, not at once. What happens if a service partner quits on the first day? That's easy. That person hasn't contributed anything and so does not become a partner. But what happens if a partner quits after contributing 90% of what was promised? Or (as is more likely) suppose a partner doesn't quit, but regularly contributes only 70% or 90% of the hours promised? These questions indicate one more type of problem you take on when you accept a service-contributing partner. Here again, there's no automatic clause to handle the issue. You have to work out what you think is fair. You may well provide for different results, depending on how nearly the service partner did as promised. When you have a meeting of the minds, write it up using or adapting the clause below.

Failure of Service Partner to Actually Perform Service

☐ If _[service partner's name]_ fails to contribute the services promised, the partnership shall proceed as follows: _[insert what you've agreed on]_ .

Future Contributions

We don't think it makes sense for you to worry now about what will happen in the future if you need more money. Adopting a partnership provision to require future cash contributions makes even less sense. If a partner doesn't have the cash needed three years from now, what good is a clause you drafted long in advance? Nevertheless, despite our views, we know some people like the sense of commitment that required future contributions provide. If you really want to require future contributions, you're not prohibited from doing so.

You can provide that additional contributions can be decided upon by a less-than-unanimous vote (perhaps a simple majority, or two-thirds vote). This isn't really feasible, however. If one partner can't—or won't—put up additional cash, it's likely to be destructive to force the issue.

In an additional contribution clause, you can add more detail, such as how notice of the need for increased capital is to be given, how much time the partners have to make the contributions, and so on.

Another way to handle the problem of needing additional cash is to have a partner, or partners, make loans to the partnership, on whatever terms the partners agree upon.

However, having a partner make loans to a business can raise a number of complicated issues. Is the loan to the partnership itself? If so, could there be a conflict between the lending partner's right to collect defaulted loans and duties of loyalty to the partnership? Or is the loan a "personal" loan to the other partners? Can a loan that the lending partner knows will ultimately be used by the borrowing partners for partnership business be reasonably called "personal"? Is interest charged on the loan? Will there be security for the loan?

 SEE AN EXPERT

See a lawyer before a partner makes loans to a partnership. As noted earlier, having a partner lend money to partners or the partnership is unusual for most beginning businesses. A complicated financial transaction like that is usually far beyond what the partners need or want. If you are seriously considering having a partner lend money to your business or to the partners individually, see a lawyer.

If you think that any future contributions may be needed, use or adapt this clause.

If Future Contributions Needed

☐ If, at any future time, more money is required to carry on the partnership business, and all partners vote to increase the capital contributions required by partners, the additional capital shall be paid in by the partners _["in equal shares" or "in the proportions as they have respectively contributed originally," etc.]_ .

Here is another type of specific clause we think is usually not warranted. It assumes that more money will be needed and that all partners will be willing and able to contribute it (without taking a vote first). In a business that will surely need more capital to expand, putting a portion of profits back into the business makes sense, but it's usually better to determine how much to contribute at the end of each year, not at the beginning. Note that if you decide to include this clause, you will have to figure out how to deal with partners who can't or won't make these additional contributions. Will you reduce the noncontributing partner's interest in the partnership and allocate it to the partners who do make capital contributions? Will you expel the noncontributing partner? Will you allow another partner to make the contribution and increase his or her interest in the partnership accordingly? Unfortunately, there's no set answer to this question: You and your fellow partners will have to sit down, figure out what seems most appropriate to your situation, and work from there.

Requirement of Annual Contribution by Partners

☐ Each person shall contribute annually _____ percent of his or her share of each year's profits [_or_ $_____] to the partnership's capital for a period of _____ years. If any partner fails to make such contribution, [_insert remedy you've decided on_].

TIP

Consider prohibiting voluntary contributions. Assuming the distribution of profits and control of the business is tied to the balances in the partners' capital accounts (for example, a one-third contribution means one-third ownership), you may want to state expressly what all should understand anyway—no partner has the right to gain more power without the others' consent by making unwanted, voluntary contributions.

No Voluntary Contributions Without Consent

☐ No partner may make any voluntary contribution to the partnership without the written consent of all other partners.

Profits, Losses, and Draws

You'll want to decide how the partnership will compensate the partners. (See Clause 5 of the partnership agreement included in this book.) After all, you're going into business to make money, so it's a good idea to figure out what will happen when you do.

The first issue here is how you'll divide profits. This can be one of the thorniest issues in creating a partnership agreement because it goes to the heart of what type of partnership you want to create. Is it the classic "all for one and one for all" of the three musketeers, with all profits shared equally, no matter what? Suppose one partner consistently brings in twice as much business as each of the others; should the "rain-making" partner be paid more? Does it matter if all the partners work equally hard, even though one brings in more money? What resentments might simmer, or erupt, if one partner is paid more or less than the others?

Next, you should determine if partners can receive a draw against their share of the profits—that is, be paid regularly, rather than only when profits are distributed. Or, you might decide that only one partner may receive a draw. This might be appropriate if one partner had less savings than the others and was counting on partnership profits to meet his or her living expenses. In theory, you could even provide that one partner gets paid a draw from contributed cash or the other partners' capital accounts, but this is quite undesirable. In effect, some partners are having their ownership share of the business eaten up to pay another.

Basic Profit/Loss Clauses

If your partnership agreement doesn't state how profits and losses are to be divided, the UPA provides that all partners share both equally, even if they contributed unequal amounts of cash, property, or labor to the partnership. If the partnership agreement defines how profits are to be distributed but doesn't mention losses, each partner must contribute toward the losses according to his or her share of profits. (UPA Section 18(a).)

If profits and losses are to be shared equally, it's better to state this expressly in your partnership agreement, rather than rely on the UPA. This will minimize any possibility of later disagreement.

Equal Shares

The partners will share all profits equally, and they will be distributed

_____[insert whatever you agreed upon, such as monthly or yearly]___ .

All losses of the partnership shall also be shared equally.

Some partnerships will choose to divide profits and losses unequally. This can be done for all sorts of reasons, such as one partner contributing more work or more money to the partnership. There's no formula that defines when you want to give partners unequal shares—it's your business and you can divide the profits and losses any way you all agree is fair.

Here are some clauses for defining the distribution of profits and losses on an unequal basis.

Unequal Shares: Set Percentages

☐ The partnership profits and losses shall be shared among the partners as follows:

Name	Percentage
_____	_____%
_____	_____%
_____	_____%

This clause is straightforward enough, but what do you do if you decide to make different allocations of profits and losses? In that situation, the following clause would be appropriate.

Unequal Shares: Different Percentages for Profits and Losses

☐ The partnership profits and losses shall be shared among the partners as follows:

Name	Percentage of Profits	Percentage of Losses
_____	_____%	_____%
_____	_____%	_____%
_____	_____%	_____%

CAUTION

Be careful if you make different allocations of profits and losses. The IRS calls these "special allocations" and they must have a legitimate purpose, or a "substantial economic effect," for the IRS to recognize them. If the IRS decides that you have made these special allocations for the sole purpose of lowering income taxes (say, by allocating all of the losses to the partner in the highest tax bracket), it will disallow the allocations. If you are interested in making different allocations of profits and losses, consult a partnership tax expert.

In some partnerships—such as investment real estate agreements—capital contributions may be the most important factor in distributing profits, especially if all partners will work in the business roughly the same amount of time. Here's a clause for this type of situation.

Unequal Shares: Profits and Losses Keyed to Capital Contributions

☐ The partnership's profits and losses shall be shared by the partners in the same proportions as their initial contributions of capital bear to each other.

Draws Paid to Partners

As mentioned, a draw is an advance of anticipated profits paid to a partner or partners. Many small business partnerships handle draws informally. If all partners decide that all can take a draw, they do. If the partners divide profits equally, each takes an equal draw. If there's an unequal division of profits, there's usually an unequal draw.

The situation is different if only some, but not all, partners receive a draw. This can be done if one partner actively works in the business and the others don't, especially if the working partner needs an ongoing income from the business. A draw can, if the business is profitable, provide this income.

> **CAUTION**
>
> **It's usually not advisable to allow draws for some partners and not others.** One reason for this is that it's hard for most new small businesses to accurately track their profits and losses on a weekly or monthly basis, so determining an appropriate figure as a draw against profits is often very difficult. If a working partner needs an income from the business, consider providing the partner with a moderate salary.

If only some partners will receive a draw, you need to state that in your agreement. We advise against specifying the amount that will be paid in draws. You cannot be sure now what your profits will be, so it's premature to contractually bind the partnership to pay partners according to a set schedule.

If despite our advice you want to authorize draws for certain partners only, here's a sample clause.

Draws Authorized

☐ Partners _____ and _____ are entitled to draws from expected partnership profits. The amount of each draw will be determined by a vote of the partners. The draws shall be paid _[insert whatever time schedule you've agreed upon, such as monthly, etc.]_ .

You can also prohibit draws. We think this is too extreme. If all partners want to take an equal draw, and the profits are there to support it, why shouldn't they? Nevertheless, there are partnerships where partners agree only to regular—say quarterly—distribution of profits and do not permit draws. In the interest of thoroughness, here's a clause prohibiting draws.

Draws Prohibited

☐ No partner shall be entitled to any draw against partnership profits. Distributions shall be made only as provided in this Agreement, or upon unanimous written agreement of the partners.

What happens if the amount a partner draws in a year turns out to exceed his or her actual share of partnership profits? Do you think you'd be able to simply ignore that fact because that partner needed all that money to live? Or does it seem fair that the partner who received more in draws have this amount treated as a loan, with an obligation to repay the partnership? Speculating over this possible problem will be unnecessary for partnerships that don't allow unequal draws. However, if you do, you may want to consider the issue.

At first, converting part of what appeared to be a draw against profits into a loan may seem harsh, but the alternative may be worse for the rest of the partners. If the partner with the excess draws can simply keep the money, you're, in effect, rewriting the basic profit distribution clause of your agreement.

If you allow unequal draws in the first place, here's a clause you can use or adapt to cover draws in excess of profits:

> *Draws Exceeding Partners' Actual Shares of Profits to Become Loans to Partners*
>
> ☐ Notwithstanding the provisions of this Agreement governing drawing permitted by partners, to the extent any partner's withdrawals for draws under those provisions during any fiscal year of the partnership exceeds his or her share in the partnership's profits, the excess shall be regarded as a loan from the partnership to him or her that he or she is obligated to repay within _____ days after the end of that fiscal year.

Retention of Profits for Business Needs

We've been asked if there's a standard percentage of profits that a partnership business should retain—for new equipment, expansions, employees' bonuses, whatever—before any remaining profits are distributed to the partners. It's a good question. Obviously, most businesses won't last long if they don't plan for the future and keep a reserve against unexpected problems. But the answer, as you might expect by now, is no, there's no set formula. Here, too, you must decide how you want your business to run. You can include a clause in your agreement to acknowledge that you'll retain some profits for future business needs. Or you can simply do it as the need arises and all agree on it.

General Limitation on Distribution to Retain Cash for Business Needs

☐ In determining the amount of profits available for distribution, allowance will be made for the fact that some money must remain undistributed and available as working capital as determined by ___*[for example,* "all partners" *or* "a majority of partners"]___ .

Here's a more mathematical approach to the problem of retaining earnings for business needs.

Specific Limitation on Distribution to Retain Cash for Business Needs

☐ The aggregate amounts distributed to the partners from the partnership profits shall not exceed _____ % of any net income above $_____.

Management Responsibilities

In this section, you'll pin down the basic ways in which you'll operate the business. This can include matters like work duties of partners (such as hours to be worked and skills contributed), supervision responsibilities, and other possible business activities permitted or prohibited to partners. Clearly, these are topics all partners will need to discuss and agree upon (see Clause 6 of the partnership agreement).

You do not need to pin down designated roles in your partnership agreement or in running your business. You are not required to have a president, vice president, treasurer, or any other officers—but of course you can have them if you want to.

A related concern is how specific to make your partnership agreement. Clauses involving management of a partnership can get very detailed, down to specifying just when office meetings should be held or what type of pens you'll buy. There's no lawyer's rule for determining how much precision is the right amount. However, we believe that it is probably best to avoid extensive detail. After all, minor matters may well change; if your computer doesn't function well and you purchase another, you don't want to have to amend your partnership agreement.

Managing the Business

You may want to specify that all, or some, of the partners will contribute specific skills, such as working as a salesperson, computer programmer, bookkeeper, or cook. If so, use or adapt the following clause:

Skills Contributed

☐ Each partner named below shall participate in the business by working in the manner described:

Partner   Type of Work

_____   _____

_____   _____

_____   _____

_____   _____

To prevent issues down the road or set expectations right away, in some situations you might want to include a clause specifying how many hours a partner is expected to work. Note that the issue of trust reappears throughout the drafting of an agreement. If you really trust your partners, do you need to specify hours worked? Maybe not, but we know of partnerships that sank into discord when one partner suddenly wasn't around much but still wanted a full share of the profits. If this occurs, you'll be glad to have your expectations in writing.

Hours Worked

☐ Except for vacations, holidays, and times of illness, each partner shall work _____ hours per week on partnership business.

Do you want to spell out what happens if a partner wants to take a leave of absence or sabbatical? Are they permitted at all? If so, how much time off is allowed? How far in advance must notice of a partner's desire to take a leave be given? Can a partner take leave no matter what the financial condition of the business? Does the partner receive any pay, or right to profits, while on leave? Must all partners approve of the leave?

Because there are so many questions here, there's very little we can give as a sample clause—just a heading and some blank lines for you to create your own leave clause.

Leaves of Absence

☐ Any partner can take a leave of absence from the partnership under the following terms and conditions:

_____

_____

_____

_____

In many small business partnerships, all the partners are involved in management and supervision (if there are any employees to supervise). This is simply stated in the agreement.

As we've said, it's generally desirable to have all partners' income be "earned" under IRS rules. This requires that each partner materially participate in the business, which the IRS defines as "regular, continuous and substantial involvement in partnership business operations." Tax law provides different tax treatment for income received from earned and passive activities. To oversimplify, receiving passive income (income from investments) can be less advantageous than receiving earned income (income from labor) for several reasons. Because most partners who participate in the partnership business generally receive earned income, there is no reason to belabor this distinction here.

All Partners Work in Business

☐ All partners shall be actively involved and materially participate in the management and operation of the partnership business.

Decisions

You should specify how management decisions are made. Many small partnerships require all decisions to be unanimous; that is, every partner has veto power.

All Decisions Unanimous

☐ Except as otherwise provided in this Agreement, all partnership decisions must be made by the unanimous agreement of all partners.

Some small business partnerships distinguish between major and minor decisions, allowing a single partner to make a minor decision but requiring unanimity for major ones. In a practical sense, you'll allow this anyway. You're not going to require a partnership meeting and vote each time a partner wants to buy a box of paper clips.

How you define major and minor decisions will depend on the personalities of the partners and type of business. Some partners adopt money as a yardstick to define the authority for each individual partner (for example, all decisions involving the expenditure or potential expenditure of more than $1,000 shall be discussed and voted on by all partners). Others handle this in some other way (that is, a decision as to what jobs to bid on, the design specifications, and the amount of the bid shall be unanimously agreed to by all partners; or decisions about the types of food to serve, particular recipes to use, and the formula by which to price catering jobs shall be agreed upon unanimously by all partners).

Major/Minor Decisions

☐ All major decisions of the partnership business must be made by a unanimous decision of all partners. Minor business decisions may be made by an individual partner. Major decisions are defined as:

_____*[write in how you've agreed to define a major decision]*_____.

Here's one example of a clause defining major decisions.

☐ The following acts may be done only with the consent of all partners:

a. Borrowing money in the partnership's name, other than in the ordinary course of the partnership's business or to finance any part of the purchase price of the partnership's properties;

b. Transferring, settling, or releasing any partnership claim, except upon payment in full;

   c. Mortgaging any partnership property, or pledging it as security for any loan;

   d. Selling or leasing any partnership property other than in the ordinary course of the partnership's business; or

   e. Knowingly causing anything to be done whereby partnership property may be seized or attached or taken in execution, or its ownership or possession otherwise be endangered.

Unequal Management Powers

In some partnerships, decision-making authority is in proportion to contributions. For example, in a partnership to purchase real estate, with little ongoing management required of the partners, a partner who put up 70% of the cash may well not want to share power equally with two partners who each put up 15%. Here are two clauses for distributing management power.

In Accordance With Contributed Capital

☐ Each partner shall participate in the management of the business. In exercising the powers of management, each partner's vote shall be in proportion to his or her interest in the partnership's capital.

By Fixed Percentage as Agreed on by Partners

☐ In the management, control, and direction of the business, the partners shall have the following percentages of voting power:

Name	Percentage
_____	_____%
_____	_____%
_____	_____%

Either of these methods may result in one partner having more than 50% of the authority in the business. With majority control, one partner can completely run the show, unless there's a specific clause requiring more than a simple majority to make decisions. Without such a clause, the minority partners may have no effective power in the business. If this is what you're considering, be careful. Are you sure it's a partnership you want? Are the minority partners really akin to investors, not owner-managers? If so, would a limited partnership or a corporation better suit their interests? (See Chapter 1.) Even the majority partner may not benefit if minority partners feel frozen out of management. A disaffected partner can always quit the partnership business, which presumably isn't what the majority partner wants—after all, why were the minority partners included in the first place?

Financial Matters

How your partnership business will deal with money is obviously something you need to talk through and reach agreement on. After that, you can be as detailed about financial matters in your agreement as you want to. Here, we look at some of the financial matters often covered in partnership agreements.

Accountings

It's wise to provide for periodic accountings so that all of the partners can keep up with partnership finances. This is especially true when some partners don't have easy access to, or ready understanding of, bookkeeping and financial records. Also, if you borrow money from a bank, the bank will likely require quarterly financial statements. Quarterly accountings should be adequate for many businesses, although others will want monthly statements. Assuming you take our advice and work with a CPA or another small business financial expert, you will want to get his or her advice on this one.

Periodic Accountings

☐ Accountings of *[specify what, such as "partners' capital accounts"*
   or "profits or losses since the last accounting"] shall be made every
   [specify time period] .

In a very small business partnership, you may well not want to
obligate yourselves to monthly or quarterly accounting, but may instead
want to handle this on a yearly basis. Still, each partner may want the
explicit right to an accounting upon request (Normally, partners have
this right under the UPA, but it's prudent to spell that out in your
agreement, so all partners are clear on the subject.)

Accounting on Request by a Partner

☐ Accountings of any aspect of partnership business shall be made upon
   written request by any partner.

At the very least, you will need to provide for a yearly accounting.

Accountant to Determine Profits and Losses

☐ The partnership's net profit or net loss for each fiscal year shall be
   determined as soon as practicable after the close of that fiscal year. This
   should be done by a certified public accountant, *[specify who, if you*
   know] , in accordance with the accounting principles employed in the
   preparation of the federal income tax return filed by the partnership
   for that year, but without a special provision for tax-exempt or partially
   tax-exempt income.

Borrowing Money

Be careful when borrowing money to establish or quickly expand a
small business, unless the partners have lots of experience running the
same type of business. Too often money borrowed to set up a business
is spent on the wrong things. In our view, it's best to borrow only for
absolutely essential items and, even then, to borrow as little as possible.

For example, leasing used equipment will cost a fraction of purchasing it new and gives you a chance to determine what you really need and what you can do without. If you do decide to borrow money, or provide for the possibility, it's best to require the consent of all partners.

Power to Borrow Money

☐ A partner can borrow money on behalf of the partnership in excess of

$_____ only with prior consent of all partners.

Expense Accounts and Partnership Checks

Will your partnership set up expense accounts for partners, which they can draw on to take clients out for dinner, pay for gas and supplies, and so on? Either way, you should include a clause in your partnership agreement addressing the issue. You should also adopt a clause indicating how many signatures are required on partnership checks. Often, partnerships require the signatures of more than one person, as a control on finances and decision making.

Expense Accounts Authorized

☐ An expense account, not to exceed $_____ per month, shall be set up for each partner for his or her actual, reasonable, and necessary expenses during the course of the business. Each partner shall keep an itemized record of these expenses and be paid once monthly for them on submission of the record.

Expense Accounts Not Authorized

☐ The partners individually and personally shall assume and pay:

- All expenses for the entertainment of persons having business relations with the partnership.
- Expenses associated with usual business activities.

Signature Required on Partnership Checks

☐ All partnership funds shall be deposited in the name of the partnership and shall be subject to withdrawal only on the signatures of at least _____ partners.

Commingling Funds

"Commingling" means mixing funds together when they should be kept separate and distinct. If a partnership business receives a check, it must go into the partnership account, not any partner's personal account. Even though this is a fundamental aspect of partnership law, it's wise to provide it explicitly.

Prohibition Against Commingling

☐ All partnership funds shall be deposited only in bank accounts bearing the partnership name.

Trust Account

A "trust account" means money one person or business controls that is legally, and morally, the property of someone else—for example, when a lawyer receives a settlement check, a portion of which belongs to a client. Money belonging to third parties should always be put in a trust, not a partnership account. Of course, many businesses will never have occasion to receive money belonging to others, so they needn't worry about this provision.

For Businesses Receiving Funds to Be Held in a Trust Account

☐ All trust and other similar funds shall be deposited in a trust account established in the partnership's name at _____ bank, and shall be kept separate and not mingled with any other funds of the partnership.

Meetings

How often do you need to meet? In most small business partnerships, you'll be meeting each other daily, maybe hourly, so do you really need a formal meeting clause? We doubt it. But if you want to specify that you'll have regular, formal meetings at time intervals that seem sensible to you (every month, every three months, and so on), there's surely no harm in doing so.

Meetings

☐ For the purpose of discussing matters of general interest to the partnership, together with the conduct of its business, partners shall meet *[describe time and days, etc.]* or at such other times agreed upon by the majority of the partners.

Records

Your agreement should indicate where the partnership will keep its books and records, and explain how partners can inspect the books. The clause below is fairly standard.

Maintenance of Records

☐ Proper and complete books of account of the partnership business shall be kept at the partnership's principal place of business and shall be open to inspection by any of the partners or their accredited representative at any reasonable time during business hours.

Vacation and Sick Leave

If you wish, you can include a clause indicating how much vacation partners can take each year, and whether that time off will be paid or not. Some partnerships prefer to handle this informally, allowing partners to take time off when they need it (and the needs of the business allow it). However, because how many hours each partner works—and takes off—can quickly become a point of contention once the business is up and running, it may be a good idea to hammer this out ahead of time.

Vacation

☐ Each partner shall be entitled to _____weeks paid [*or unpaid*] vacation per year.

Do you want to make an express provision governing what will happen if a partner becomes seriously ill? This is a subject you should discuss, of course. But how can you know now how you'd want to handle it if it occurs? There are so many variables, including the needs of the ill partner, the income of the business, and the duration of the illness. However, if you decide you do want a provision, at least a general one, stating you do or do not allow sick leave, you can include it here.

Sick Leave

☐ The partnership's sick leave policy for partners is _____

_____

_____

_____

_____.

Outside Business Activities

A key partnership question is whether any partner can engage in outside business. Often, of course, they must, at least at first, because the partnership business income is unlikely to be sufficient to support the partners. If a partner can engage in outside business, what types are permitted? Allowing a partner to directly compete with the partnership obviously risks serious conflicts of interest. But if you prohibit directly competitive businesses, how do you determine what is direct competition? If the partners are running a restaurant, can a partner be an owner of a delicatessen? Work in a delicatessen?

Remember, the first priority is that each partner must be able to survive financially while the partnership business has time to become profitable. This is an important area to cover, because people can feel vital interests are at stake, including the integrity of the partnership and the ability to make enough money to live, or live comfortably. So take the time to talk this out and be sure you all agree on what clauses like "materially interfere with the partnership business" mean. Surprises and misunderstandings here can lead to much unpleasantness among the partners.

Here are four clauses for different approaches to this issue.

Permitted, Except for Direct Competition

☐ Any partner may be engaged in one or more other businesses as well as the business of the partnership, but only to the extent that this activity does not directly and materially interfere with the business of the partnership and does not conflict with the time commitments and other obligations of that partner to the partnership under this Agreement. Neither the partnership nor any other partner shall have any right to any income or profit derived by a partner from any business activity permitted under this section.

Permitted

☐ It is understood and agreed that each partner may engage in other businesses, including enterprises in competition with the partnership. The partners need not offer any business opportunities to the partnership, but may take advantage of those opportunities for their own accounts or for the accounts of other partnerships or enterprises with which they are associated. Neither the partnership nor any other partner shall have any right to any income or profit derived by a partner from any enterprise or opportunity permitted by this section.

Specific Activities Permitted

☐ The list below specifies business activities that each partner plans or may do outside of the partnership business. Each partner is expressly authorized to engage in these activities if he or she so desires:

_____

_____

_____.

Restricted

☐ As long as any person is a member of the partnership, he or she shall devote his or her full work time and energies to the conduct of partnership business, and shall not be actively engaged in the conduct of any other business for compensation or a share in profits as an employee, officer, agent, proprietor, partner, or stockholder. This prohibition shall not prevent him or her from being a passive investor in any enterprise, however, if he or she is not actively engaged in its business and does not exercise control over it. Neither the partnership nor any other partner shall have any right to any income or profit derived from any such passive investment.

Ownership of Business Assets

If a partner leaves or the partnership dissolves, it's vital to know who owns the partnership's assets. The question here is: Was the asset owned by the partnership or by an individual partner? Obviously, property that is held in the partnership name—real estate, a car, and so on—is partnership property. But what of more sophisticated types of property, such as trade secrets, patents, copyrights, or the partnership name itself (which, as we've noted, can be very important to many businesses, from restaurants to fashion designers)? Here are clauses that state that certain assets are partnership property. You can adapt or modify any of these clauses to suit your needs.

Trade Secrets

☐ All trade secrets used or developed by the partnership, including customer lists and sources of supplies, will be owned and controlled by the partnership.

Patents

☐ Any ideas developed by one or more partners pertaining to partnership business that are the subject of an application for a patent shall be partnership property.

Copyrights

☐ All copyrighted materials in the partnership name are, and shall remain, partnership property.

Business Name

☐ The partnership business name of __[specify]__ shall be partnership property. In the event of the departure of a partner and/or dissolution of the partnership, control and ownership of the partnership business name shall be determined pursuant to this Agreement.

Provision for a Managing Partner

Managing partners are common in large partnerships, such as big restaurants or service businesses. Especially if some or most of the partners don't want to be involved in day-to-day management, you'll need a managing partner. Having a managing partner can be appropriate if all or most of the partners will work in the business in other capacities (for example, ten architects choose one as the managing partner). However, if most partners won't work in the business, they may want to consider a limited partnership instead of a general partnership with a managing partner. One big advantage is that the financial liability of a limited partner is limited to the amount of his or her contribution, while a general partner in a partnership with a managing partner has unlimited financial liability. We realize that most of our readers aren't in this situation, but for those few who are, we offer several possible clauses. First, here is a clause where the managing partner has wide powers.

Authority of Managing Partner

☐ The managing partner shall be __[name]__. The managing partner shall have control over the business of the partnership and assume direction of its business operations. The managing partner shall consult and confer as far as practicable with the nonmanaging partners, but the power of decision shall be vested in the managing partner. The managing partner's power and duties shall include control over the partnership's books and records and hiring any independent certified public accountant the managing partner deems necessary for this purpose. On the managing partner's death, resignation, or other disability, a new managing partner shall be selected by a majority of the partners.

Next is a clause granting more limited power to the managing partner. To make this work, you'll need to define what a "major" or "basic" partnership business decision is.

Limited Authority for Managing Partner

☐ The managing partner shall be __[name]__. The managing partner shall have control over routine business transactions and day-to-day operating decisions. The managing partner shall not make any major or basic decisions without consent of a majority of the partners. A major or basic decision is defined as _[state the definition you've agreed on]_.

Salary of Managing Partner

☐ The managing partner shall be paid a monthly salary of $_____ or such other amount that may be determined by the unanimous written agreement of the partners. This salary shall be treated as a partnership expense in determining its profits or losses.

Managing Partner Handles All Money of the Partnership

☐ All partnership funds shall be deposited in the partnership's name and shall be subject to withdrawal only on the signature of the managing partner.

Managing Partner Handles Operating Fund Only

☐ All partnership funds shall be deposited in the partnership's name and shall be subject to withdrawal only on the signatures of at least _____ partners, except that a separate account may be maintained with a balance never to exceed $_____. The amounts in that separate account shall be subject to withdrawal on the signature of the managing partner. ●

Changes and Growth of Your Partnership

I n this chapter, we focus on anticipating and planning for business growth. You and your partners want to explore how compatible your plans for the business are. How much do you each want your business to grow? How much income does each partner hope for? Do you want employees?

We think it is not sensible to try to pin down every detail at this point. But whatever you decide about the growth of your business, you'll surely have to deal with change. Your partnership agreement should address at least two concerns involving change and growth. First, you'll want a clause stating how your agreement can be amended. Second, you should focus now on the possibility of admitting a new partner and figure out what procedures you'll follow to take someone into your partnership. These two concerns are covered in Clause 7 of the partnership agreement included in this book.

Amending the Partnership Agreement

Some types of business growth will necessitate a change in your partnership agreement. For example, adding a new partner will require revisions of (at least) the clauses listing the partners' names and those covering contributions and distribution of profits. It may also require other changes to your agreement.

Even if you don't admit any new partners, business growth may require changes in your partnership agreement. You and your partners may decide that the expanded business should be run differently than the original business. Or perhaps the business will need additional cash contributions, and you'll decide that they should be made in proportions different from those originally agreed to. Any significant change in the structure or operation of your business should be reflected by a change in the partnership agreement. Just what amounts to a significant change is up to you to decide. Some changes, such as an alteration in the distribution of profits a partner receives or assets a partner contributes, are obviously significant. Others, such as the decision to have more formal partnership meetings or change the accounting protocol, may or may not seem significant enough to you to warrant changing your partnership agreement.

The important thing is that you have rules about how your agreement can be amended. The great majority of small business partnerships require written consent by all partners to amend the agreement. This is simply one application of a basic partnership philosophy requiring unanimity.

Here's a sample clause permitting amendment only if all partners agree.

By Unanimous Agreement

☐ This Agreement may be amended only by written consent of all partners.

Partnership Mergers

Two distinct partnerships can merge and become one. Recently, this has been occurring rather often when two large law firms become one yet-larger firm. Complex IRS provisions apply to partnership mergers. Discussing these provisions is beyond the scope of this book. If you become involved in a partnership merger, you'll need a lawyer knowledgeable in this field. Indeed, you almost surely already have one.

In theory, you can create any amendment clause you desire. You could specify that the agreement could be amended by a vote of 51% of the partners, or by 51% of the capital accounts. We believe it's unwise for small business partnerships to allow their agreements to be amended by less than a unanimous vote of the partners, however. Other methods could leave one or more partners powerless—the dominant partners could simply amend the original agreement out of existence. This could leave the powerless partners with no recourse except to quit the partnership.

TIP

You may want to modify the rule of unanimity for amending the agreement if you're setting up a large partnership. We know of some collective businesses, for example, where there are 15, 20, and even 30 partners. In this situation it may make sense to allow a change in the agreement if, say, 75% of the partners approve. However, many collectives or large partnerships, such as good-sized accounting or architecture firms, still retain the requirement of unanimous consent to change the agreement.

If you want to allow amendments by less than unanimity, choose the following clause:

As Specified

☐ This Agreement may be amended by ___ [*whatever method you've decided upon*] ___ .

Admission of a New Partner

Now let's focus on one specific aspect of growth that you should definitely handle in your original partnership agreement—the admission of a new partner or partners. Growth of a partnership business may lead to the opportunity, or even the necessity, of taking in a new partner or partners for any of a number of reasons. To name a few of the more common ones:

- desire (or need) for the new partner's contribution of cash
- need for skills contributed by the new partner
- need for additional management
- need to retain a key employee by allowing him or her to become a partner, or
- desire to expand your business to new locations or customers offered by the new partner.

Adding a new partner is such a vital issue that it's better not to rely on your general amendment clause to cover it. Instead, state expressly in your partnership agreement how a new partner can be admitted. The major question to face is whether all existing partners have to agree to do this. We believe that it's wise to require unanimous consent, particularly in small partnerships.

Addition by Unanimous Written Agreement of All Partners

☐ A new partner or partners may be added to the partnership only by unanimous written consent of all existing partners.

Admitting a New Partner to Large Partnerships

If a large partnership requires unanimity to admit a new partner, there can be serious problems if one or more partners refuse to accept the majority decision. Most larger partnerships we know (mostly big cooperatives) have nevertheless handled this issue by specifying in their agreement that unanimity is required for admission of a new partner. The truth is, conflicts over admitting a new partner are rare. And, there are ways to test out a potential partner to see if he or she will fit in. For example, one food sales collective we know of invites prospective partners to work for the enterprise for several weeks. After that time, the partners vote on whether the newcomer will be accepted into the business. If it's unanimous, the hours he or she has worked are credited toward his or her buy-in amount. However, if the partners reject the prospective partner after this try-out period, the partners pay him or her for this work at the going rate (agreed upon before they start).

Further, if one or a few partners of a large partnership attempt to regularly thwart the will of the majority regarding the admission of new partners, peer pressure can often curtail this obstructionism. If peer pressure fails, large partnerships almost invariably have expulsion provisions in their agreement, so a partner who consistently or arbitrarily stands alone, preventing new partners from being admitted, may eventually be thrown out.

If, despite our advice, a large partnership decides that less than unanimous consent will be required to admit a new partner, here's a clause you can use or adapt to accomplish that goal.

Addition by Less Than All Partners

☐ A new partner may be admitted to the partnership with the written approval of _[state method agreed upon—for example, partners holding 75% of the capital interest of the partnership; or, 80% of the votes of the partners, etc., or whatever you decide]_ .

Adding a New Partner When You've Failed to Plan Ahead

How do you proceed if you have nothing but an oral partnership agreement, or a written one that simply doesn't provide for the admission of a new partner? Assuming that you and your partners have talked it over and are in agreement on future actions, now is the time to draft a comprehensive partnership agreement. If you can't agree on future plans, things won't be so simple; the fact that you have no written agreement —including a procedure to handle disagreements—will almost surely aggravate your problem. Bluntly put, if you can't at least agree on a mechanism to arrive at an agreement, there's little you can do except dissolve your partnership.

If, however, you do agree to expand and want to admit a new partner, this can be an excellent time to review your partnership agreement. If possible, you will want to replace whatever existing understanding you have with a written agreement that is both current and comprehensive. In a sense, you are in the same position as people adopting an agreement for the first time. One nice thing about a partnership—as opposed to a corporation—is that it can be changed easily at any time all partners agree. To clarify the situation, you could begin the new partnership agreement with a general introductory clause, such as the following:

Admitting a New Partner When You've Failed to Plan Ahead

☐   _[Names of old partners]_ have been engaged in business at ___[location]___ as a partnership under the firm name of _____. They now intend to admit _[name of new partner]_ to their partnership, and all the members of the expanded partnership desire to amend and clarify the terms and conditions of their Partnership Agreement and to reduce their agreement to writing.

Dissolution of the Partnership When a New Partner Joins

Admitting a new partner causes a technical "dissolution" of the original partnership. A dissolution of a partnership need not imply the sort of negative consequences that we associate with the term "dissolution of marriage" (that is, termination of the relationship). In the context of adding a new partner, a partnership "dissolution" is simply the legal term used for a change in the membership of the partnership. Even if the business otherwise continues as usual, there has been a technical dissolution of the old partnership and the simultaneous continuation of that business by the newly created partnership. In other situations, however, the dissolution of a partnership may signal a much more fundamental change—up to and including the partnership's ceasing to do business. Continuing a partnership without dissolution when a new partner is added or a partner leaves is further discussed in "Continuing the Partnership" in Chapter 5.

Legally, from the moment of dissolution of a partnership business, no new partnership business can be undertaken by the old partnership. The original partners have legal authority only to wind up the business as rapidly as is feasible. (UPA Sections 30, 33, 35, and 37.) In the case of the addition of a new partner, however, the "dissolution" of the old partnership is basically a technical matter. The major problem is to close out an old set of books and start another. The business itself can go happily on. To make this clear, use the following clause in the section of your agreement on admitting a new partner:

No Dissolution of the Partnership When a New Partner Joins

☐ Admission of a new partner shall not cause dissolution of the underlying partnership business, which will be continued by the new partnership entity.

The Incoming Partner's Liability for Existing Partnership Debts

Most of the issues the partners must deal with when a new partner is welcomed to your business family are the same as those that you resolved in your original partnership agreement—who gets what, who contributes what, and who does what. However, one important additional matter must be resolved. Will the incoming partner be personally responsible for the existing debts of the partnership? Under the Uniform Partnership Act, a new partner is personally liable for partnership debts incurred before he or she became a partner, up to his or her share of (that is, contribution to) partnership property. (UPA Section 17.) Of course, once someone becomes a partner, he or she has unlimited personal liability for partnership debts incurred after his or her admission to the partnership.

EXAMPLE: Raul contributes $50,000 when he joins Elaine and Beverly in a partnership to produce pet food. When Raul joins the partnership, the two women owe $100,000. Raul's maximum liability for the preexisting debts would be the $50,000 he contributes.

The partners can vary this rule in the partnership agreement. This means that Beverly and Elaine could agree to release Raul from any liability for partnership debts that existed before he became a partner. Even so, the $50,000 he put up would be part of the business, and creditors could go after it if the business had no other assets. Or, at the other extreme, Raul could assume full personal liability for all existing debts. But to do this, Raul must clearly assume such liability.

Whatever the legal rules, it is risky to join a partnership that has substantial debts. Creditors tend to sue anyone who's an owner of an insolvent business, no matter when the owner came on board. Whether you're a new incoming partner or a member of the original partnership, you undoubtedly hope that existing debts will be an academic problem and that your business is sufficiently profitable to pay debts from operating revenues. But, of course, this isn't always true. Indeed, one reason to bring in a new partner is precisely because the old partners need more cash. This is one example of how it's impractical to put detailed future plans in your partnership agreement before you start the business. It's impossible to know what sort of debt situation you will face two years from now. Sure, you could put a clause in your original agreement saying that all new partners must be ready to assume personal liability for all partnership debts no matter when incurred, but what good does that do? What happens if the only suitable person you can find balks? A custom-tailored clause regarding a new partner's liability for existing debts is likely to be necessary, so there's no point in trying to anticipate the problem before you face it (which you may well never need to do).

Here are three clauses for handling the issue of partnership debts and the incoming partner. The first limits the incoming partner's liability; the second states the UPA rule that the incoming partner is liable for existing debts up to his or her investment in the business; and the third imposes maximum liability by providing the incoming partner is responsible for all partnership debts, no matter when the partnership incurred them.

Not Responsible for Partnership Debts Before Becoming Partner

☐ _____*[Incoming partner]*_____ shall not be personally responsible for, or assume any liability for, any debts of __*[name of partnership business]*__ incurred on or before _____, 20____.

Responsible for Partnership Debts From Set Date

☐ _____*[Incoming partner]*_____ hereby expressly assumes personal liability for debts of _____*[name of partnership business]*_____ incurred on or before _____, 20_____, equal to the amount of his or her contribution to the partnership, totaling $_____.

Responsible for All Partnership Debts

☐ ___[Incoming partner]___ hereby expressly assumes full personal liability equal to the personal liability of all other partners in the partnership of ___[name of partnership business]___ for all partnership debts and obligations whenever incurred.

Tax Liability of Incoming Partners

If a new partner receives a capital (that is, equity) interest in a partnership in exchange for services rendered or to be rendered to the partnership, that partner will be taxed immediately for the fair market value of the interest received. (The interest the partner receives must be without substantial risk of forfeiture for this tax rule to apply. Cases where there is a substantial risk of forfeiture are somewhat rare—they include instances where the partnership property has already been liened by a creditor.) This can be a real problem for newly admitted partners to professional partnerships, because the new partner will probably receive an interest in the (taxable) assets of the partnership, including accounts receivable and earned (but unbilled) fees.

> **EXAMPLE:** Phillip and Betty operate a successful accounting firm. They decide to invite Janice, who has worked for them for years, to join their partnership because she's a good worker and a good friend, but also because they fear that if they don't give her a better deal, she'll open her own competing business. Janice receives 25% interest in the partnership and is not required to pay anything for it. The partners calculate the fair market value of this interest to be worth $100,000. Although Janice doesn't receive $100,000 cash—just her ownership interest in the business assets (that is, fixed assets, accounts receivable, unbilled fees, and goodwill)—the IRS takes the position that she's received ordinary income amounting to $100,000, which is subject to income tax. In sum, come tax payment time, Janice will be out of pocket a substantial amount because she received her partnership ownership interest.

Because of this harsh tax rule (and often because it makes practical sense as well), it can be wiser for a service partner to sign a contract with the partnership that she'll receive her ownership (equity) interest in the business over time, as services are performed. Or perhaps the partnership will agree to pay the taxes. But as we discuss in Chapter 8, it's not easy to solve this problem so that all partners are fully satisfied, and you'll likely need to consult an accountant or other tax adviser experienced with partnership tax issues.

Outgoing Partners

We discuss the problems caused by departure of a partner in Chapter 5. Here we just want to remind you that it's not unusual for the admission of a new partner to a business to coincide with the departure of another.

Problems caused by the departure of a partner are usually much more complicated than admission of a new partner. Normally, unless the new partner directly purchases the departing partner's interest, that interest must be valued. Arrangements are often made by the remaining partners to buy that interest. Clauses specifying how this is to be handled should be in the original partnership agreement, so be sure to check the next chapter carefully. Also, remember that outgoing partners remain personally liable to the business's creditors for all debts of the partnership incurred up to the time they leave. As we've said, an incoming partner may or may not assume personal responsibility for those debts. But even if an incoming partner does assume full responsibility for old partnership debts, this doesn't release the departing partner from potential liability to existing creditors. Likewise, even a written release and assumption of liability by the new partner for the old partner doesn't automatically leave the old partner in the clear. If all the partners (including the new one) are broke, creditors of the old partnership can still go after the departed partner.

EXAMPLE: Al and James are partners in A-J Auto Body Repair. Al leaves, selling his partnership interest to Peter, who assumes personal liability for all existing debts of A-J. On the date Al leaves, A-J owes $36,000 to Nifty Paints, a major paint supplier. A-J never pays the bill, and six months later, the business goes broke. Neither James nor Peter has any personal assets. Al can be held liable by Nifty for the full $36,000 owed. Of course, Al has a claim for this amount against Peter (who assumed that debt); but if Peter is broke, it doesn't seem likely Al will collect on it. ●

Changes: Departure of a Partner, Buyouts, and Business Continuation

This is very likely the most important chapter in this book, yet it's one that many people will be tempted to skim. When you're excited and full of energy about establishing a new business, it probably seems unnecessary, or even destructive, to worry about a partner leaving. But you owe it to yourselves to consider what you'll do if one of you voluntarily leaves, becomes disabled or dies, or is even expelled from the partnership. These and related issues are covered in Clauses 8, 9, and 10 of the partnership agreement included in this book.

Sooner or later the makeup of your partnership will change. A partner may want to leave for all sorts of reasons—to start another business, to move to Paris, to teach yoga. Or, if you all stay together for many years, a partner will inevitably retire or die. However a partner leaves, the same fundamental issues come up. To whom can the departing partner sell his or her interest? Do the remaining partners, or partner, have the right to buy it before anyone else can? How is the purchase price determined? Can the departing partner force the remaining partners to buy his or her interest, if no outside buyer can be found? What happens to the partnership business when a partner leaves? What are the departing partner's rights and duties to the remaining partners and partnership business? Finally, what happens if the partnership ends because all partners agree to do so?

It's simply not good business sense to leave these questions open and unresolved. If you haven't adopted procedures to deal with them, there's a serious risk of conflict. A departing partner's interest is often directly opposed to that of those who remain, because the departing partner often wants a much higher price for his or her interest than the remaining partners think it is worth. And if, as has been known to happen, either side or both sides harbor grievances against the other, matters can become dangerously hostile and conflicted.

You need to reach agreement about three basic issues:

- Does the partnership or the remaining partners have the right, or even the obligation, to buy a departing partner's interest? This is called a "buy-sell" agreement.

- If there is no outside buyer, how is the value of a departing partner's interest determined?
- How are payments to a departing partner made?

In hashing out your views and writing down your decisions about a departing partner, you'll be making rules for your shared endeavor—rules that are legally enforceable. This is a valuable security to have, even if you all remain partners for decades.

Now let's look at some examples of problems that can arise if a partner leaves a partnership:

- Does the remaining partner have the right to buy the departing partner's interest? If so, how is the purchase price determined?
- Does the reason for quitting matter? Would you be willing to pay the same amount as a buyout price whether your partner becomes ill with rheumatoid arthritis or runs off to Hawaii?
- What happens if the departing partner wants to sell to someone you don't know, or even worse, someone you do know and can't stand?
- Can a partner take a leave of absence? If so, can you expel a partner who stays away too long?
- What happens if a partner becomes disabled and can no longer work in the business? Who determines that a partner has become disabled within the meaning of your partnership agreement?
- What happens if your partner becomes mentally ill, gets Alzheimer's, or is killed?
- What happens if one of your partners becomes alcohol or drug dependent, and can no longer make sound business decisions?
- Suppose your partner gets divorced and his or her spouse ends up with a share of the business as part of a property settlement. If they're not speaking, what do you do?
- What if the partners all want to end the partnership, but each wants to continue the business on their own?
- What happens if a partner dies and his or her spouse wants to cash in as fast as possible?

To prepare sensible partnership clauses governing partners' departures, go though this chapter carefully: talk, discuss, argue, speculate—do everything you can to pin down what seems fair if a partner leaves. Today, no one knows if he or she will be the person who wants to leave or a person who wants to stay, so all partners should look at the question from both positions.

Buy-Sell Clauses

In this section, we'll cover issues concerning the sale of a departing partner's interest in the business, including:
- the right of the remaining partners to buy that interest
- what happens if the remaining partners decline to buy that interest
- requiring advance notice of withdrawal, and
- conflicts regarding which partner can buy out which others.

Sometimes buy-sell agreements, especially when they're very complex, are prepared as separate documents. We see no reason for this additional paperwork in most cases. You should be able to keep your buy-sell agreement succinct enough so it can be included in your partnership agreement.

To avoid the scary possibility that an unwanted person might buy, or otherwise acquire, a departing partner's share of a business, most buy-sell agreements contain what's called a "right of first refusal." This clause requires a departing partner to offer his or her share to the remaining partners before selling or transferring it to anyone else. (If you've ever dealt in real estate, it's kind of like buying an option on a building.)

 **SEE AN EXPERT**

Right-to-buy agreements may not be enforceable in the context of a partner's death. In a few states, buyout agreements were held void in cases where one partner died, on the grounds that the agreement was "testamentary in character" and did not conform to the state law on wills. Check the laws in your state.

The Right of First Refusal

Do you want to allow a partner to be able to freely sell or transfer his or her partnership interest to an outsider no matter what the other partners want? Your answer should probably be no. You need a very persuasive reason (we can't think of one) to exclude a right of first refusal clause from your agreement. If one partner leaves, the remaining partners normally want at least an option to buy the departing partner's share and continue the business. Otherwise, if one partner withdraws, there can be unfortunate consequences, such as:

- The business may have to be liquidated. Selling off your used computers, machinery, and the sofa in the waiting room, isn't going to make much money for anybody. Most businesses are worth far more as operating entities than they are as carcasses up for sale to the highest bidder.
- The withdrawing partner may attempt to sell or transfer his or her interest without all partners' consent. Obviously this raises the possibility of all sorts of unhappy scenarios.

To avoid these unwanted possibilities, a well-drafted partnership agreement normally contains a right of first refusal clause. This clause guarantees that a departing partner who receives a good-faith offer from an outside buyer will be able to get that price, either from the partners or the outside person. Using this term in your agreement prohibits a partner from getting an unreasonably high dummy bid to jack up the sale price to the remaining partners.

Some partners decide that they do not want to have a right of first refusal clause in their agreement. Instead, they provide that a departing partner's interest shall be valued only as determined under a method set forth in their agreement. (The different methods for doing this are set forth in "Determining the Value of the Business," below.) They believe that if a partner leaves, it makes more sense to keep the remaining partners happy and functioning, even if the departing partner could have received a higher price by selling to an outsider. This means the remaining partners can never be forced into business with someone they don't like. Of course, if the time comes, the remaining partners could still permit the departing partner to sell to an outsider if they did like this new person. There is, after all, a real incentive for this—the remaining partners won't have to pay any money (from the business or from their own personal assets) to the departing partner.

But most partnerships decide that it is too unfair to a departing partner to deny him or her a higher price offered by a bona fide buyer. So they include a right of first refusal clause in their partnership agreement. If you want one in your agreement, use or adapt the one below. To complete the clause, you need to agree upon and then insert the number of days the partnership has, after it's been notified of the outside offer, to buy the departing partner's interest.

The Right of First Refusal Upon Offer From Outsider

☐ If any partner receives a bona fide, legitimate offer, whether or not solicited by him or her, from any person to purchase all of his or her interest in the partnership, and if the partner receiving the offer is willing to accept it, he or she shall give written notice of the amount and terms of the offer, the identity of the proposed buyer, and his or her willingness to accept the offer to each of the other partners. The other partner or partners shall have the option, within _____ days after the notice is given, to purchase that partner's interest on the same terms as those contained in the offer.

RESOURCE

Want more information on buyouts? More detailed provisions for buy-sell clauses are contained in *Business Buyout Agreements*, by Anthony Mancuso and Bethany Laurence (Nolo). For example, if you want a specific clause on buyouts if a partner becomes disabled, covering such matters as how disability is defined and how long a disability must exist before a buyout can or must occur, you'll find it in *Business Buyout Agreements*.

SEE AN EXPERT

Right of first refusal clauses can get complicated very quickly. You could include provisions requiring extensive details about any outside offer and would-be buyer, plus precise requirements for what makes an offer "bona fide," as well as what happens if a departing partner wants to sell only to one remaining partner (not to the partnership itself) and whether a partner can make gifts of his or her interest. Here we provide a clause that covers the basics, which should cover the needs of a beginning partnership. If you want to create a clause that goes into considerable detail and covers many contingencies, you'll likely need to see a lawyer.

The Right of the Partnership to Buy a Partner's Interest

The right of first refusal clause only applies if a departing partner receives a bona fide outside offer. But suppose a departing partner doesn't get any outside offer? Or suppose a partner leaves because of disability or death, or goes bankrupt or is expelled? Or suppose a partner's interest, or a portion of it, is transferred by gift, by agreement between the partner and an outsider, or by court order, as in a divorce case? Then what? In all these cases, the remaining partners will normally want the right to buy, at their option, the interest of a departing partner.

Below, we provide a right-to-buy clause. Under this clause, the partnership has the right to buy the interest of a departing partner, no matter what the reason for the departure. An outsider who receives a share of a business has no right to force her- or himself into the partnership. The outsider must sell the interest back to the partnership, assuming the partnership enforces the clause, which is not mandatory for the partnership. The remaining partners could decide, if they wish, to take the outsider in as a new partner. This is an example, and a reminder, that rules in a partnership agreement don't have to be binding if none of the partners want them to be. Agreement rules should protect partners and define their rights, not freeze them in a legal straightjacket.

What happens if someone receives a share of the business and would prefer not to be bought out by the remaining partners? First, realize that this is unlikely. How often does a person insist on becoming a member of a business against the wishes of the other owners? (Especially when the alternative is to receive money for the ownership interest.) On balance, we feel it's best to protect the existing partners and partnership from being compelled to accept a co-owner they don't want.

The following clause allows the partners to buy in any case, except when a right of first refusal applies.

Sale to Partnership or Partners at Their Option

☐ If any partner leaves the partnership, for whatever reason, whether he or she quits, withdraws, is expelled, retires, becomes mentally or physically incapacitated or unable to fully function as a partner, or dies, or if the partner attempts to or is ordered to transfer his or her interest, whether voluntarily or involuntarily, he or she, or his or her estate, shall be obligated to sell his or her interest in the partnership to the remaining partner or partners, who have the option, but not the obligation, to buy that interest. However, if the departing partner receives a bona fide offer from a prospective outside buyer, the Right of First Refusal Clause of this Agreement shall apply.

Drafting Two-Person Partnership Clauses

The preceding clause refers to a partnership or partners that remain after one partner leaves. But if there were only two partners originally, and one departs, there's only one partner left—so there can't be "remaining partners" left. Therefore, when drafting an agreement for a two-person partnership, you must vary the sample clauses to refer to the "remaining owner," or "remaining partner" as shown below. Similarly, two-person partnerships should vary the sample clauses throughout this book to refer to the remaining owner rather than the partnership, when only one person will remain if a partner leaves.

The preceding clause for a two-person partnership should read as follows:

Sale to Partner at His or Her Option

☐ If either partner leaves the partnership, for whatever reason, whether he or she quits, withdraws, retires, becomes mentally or physically incapacitated or unable to fully function as a partner, or dies, or if the partner attempts to or is ordered to transfer his or her interest, whether voluntarily or involuntarily, he or she, or his or her estate, shall be obligated to sell his or her interest in the partnership to the remaining owner, who has the option, but not the obligation, to buy that interest. However, if the departing partner receives a bona fide offer from a prospective outside buyer, the Right of First Refusal Clause of this Agreement shall apply.

Forced Buyouts

What happens if a partner leaves and cannot find an outside buyer? What happens if a partner leaves for any reason, and the remaining partners don't want to buy out that departing partner's interest? If there's no clause governing the refusal of the remaining partner or partners to buy, the departing partner may be stuck.

An entire business is often much more saleable than a share of that business. So if the remaining partners refuse to buy the interest of a departing partner, the best solution, at least from the departing partner's point of view, is to sell the whole business and divide the proceeds. This gives the remaining partners a choice—buy the departing partner's share of the business or lose their own. An important decision here is how long the remaining partners have to make up their minds after the departing one is gone. A common period is six months. That gives them a reasonable time to see how the business works without the departing partner. But you are definitely free to choose any time period you all agree on.

Here is a clause covering refusal-to-buy:

Refusal of Remaining Partners to Buy

☐ If the remaining partner or partners do not purchase the departing partner's share of the business, under the terms provided in this Agreement, within [*time period after the departing partner leaves*], the entire business of the partnership shall be put up for sale, and listed with the appropriate sales agencies, agents, or brokers.

Notice that this clause does not cover outside buyers, because it doesn't have to. If the partnership agreement contains a right of first refusal clause and there's an outside buyer, then the departing partner can sell to that buyer, unless the remaining partners exercise their option. So this clause comes into play only if no outside buyer for one partner's share can be found. And if the partnership agreement prohibits the departing partner from reselling to an outside buyer, then it doesn't matter if one appears.

There's another approach to the refusal-to-buy problem, which is to have a clause compelling the remaining partners to buy, called a "forced buyout." In theory, this protects a departing owner from being stuck with a partnership interest. But this drastic solution may not be workable. If the remaining partners don't have the cash and are unwilling or unable to borrow it, how can they be made to pay for the departing partner's interest? Even if they could pay for it, if they choose not to, what will happen if a departing partner attempts to force a buyout? At best, dragged-out negotiations, conflict, and slow payments. At worst, a lawsuit attempting to enforce a forced buyout clause, then more legal work to enforce any court judgment. And looming over all these hassles are two clichés that remain distressingly true: Possession is nine-tenths of the law, and you can't get blood from a stone.

We think a far more desirable way to handle the reluctance or refusal of the remaining partners to buy is a clause requiring the forced sale of the entire business. This forces the remaining partners to face up to a financial reality: Either they let the business go, or they buy out the departing partner's interest. But they cannot simply ignore a partner who wants out.

Advance Notice of Withdrawal

Many partnerships decide they want advance notice, if possible, before a partner leaves. Obviously, this isn't possible if a partner suddenly becomes seriously injured, mentally incompetent, or dies, but the vast majority of partner departures are not caused by illness, disability, or death but by a desire or need to move on. In that case, a sensible advance notice clause seems fair. Of course, you get to decide how long a lead time is required.

What's the sanction if a partner doesn't comply with a notice clause? Whatever you want. A common one is to provide, when you get to valuation of the business, that the value of a departing partner's share who violates the notice provision will be reduced by a set percentage, such as 10% or 20%. Or, when inadequate notice is given, you can provide for a longer time for payment of the buyout price. Usually, you can't define your sanction until you've been through the subsequent sections of this chapter. For now, simply provide that the sanction is "as provided elsewhere in this Agreement." But be sure you actually write in that sanction elsewhere, and don't simply forget about it later on.

What happens if you have an advance notice clause and a partner has an emergency and feels he or she has to leave suddenly? Well, first remember that you don't have to enforce any partnership clause, including this one. If all partners agree that it's fair to waive it, you can. But if one or more partners want to enforce the notice clause, it's important that all understand that, whatever the departing partner's emergency, the remaining partners have been surprised and must carry on the business without being properly warned of the changes they'll have to cope with. So they can fairly insist that they should be compensated for this burden by paying the departing partner a lower buyout price. After all, here the departing partner is moving on to greener, or at least richer, pastures, and should be able to absorb some financial cost.

Requiring Advance Notice of Withdrawal

☐ Unless physically prevented from giving notice, a partner shall give

[time period] written advance notice of his or her intention to leave

the partnership. If he or she fails to do so _[describe the sanction imposed]_ .

Conflicts Regarding Right to Buy

Now let's examine some possible conflicts regarding right-to-buy provisions and look at clauses designed to cope with them. What happens if two equal partners (or an equal number of partners on both sides) can't get along, and each wants to buy the other out? How do the partners decide who has the right to buy? The obvious answer is that it can't be decided, unless you've previously created some clause to resolve this question or, when the problem develops, you work out some sort of compromise acceptable to both. If you have no prearranged agreement, and neither side will compromise, under the terms of the UPA the business will have to be liquidated and the net proceeds distributed to the ex-partners. If there's a buyout conflict in a multimember partnership, it's possible that the majority could expel the minority (if allowed in the agreement) and then buy out their interest under the agreement. This is obviously a drastic solution, and the bitterness created will surely damage the business.

In a two-person or even-member partnership, there's a real possibility of a deadlock. To prevent a forced sale, you can adopt any reasonable method to see who leaves and who stays. Commonly used methods include the coin flip and auction bidding.

The coin flip method may seem simplistic, but nevertheless lots of partnerships use it because it has the great virtue of simplicity: "Heads I get to buy, tails you do." (Do be sure you all trust whoever flips the coin.)

The Coin Flip

☐ If the partners cannot agree on who has the right to purchase the other

partners' interest in the business, that right shall be determined by the flip

of a coin [to be flipped by _____[name]_____].

With auction bidding, each side offers a price for the business, and can then bid their price up, until the higher bid wins.

EXAMPLE: Bob and Skip each tire of the other and decide to end their boat/ marina partnership. Bob wants very much to continue the business. He and Skip both believe the market value for their business is roughly $320,000 to $340,000. Bob offers to buy Skip's share of the business at $166,000, figuring Skip will decide to sell because Bob's price is toward the high side. But Skip counters with $169,000 for Bob's share. Now Bob has to decide whether to bid near maximum for the business or cash out. Bob's a gambler, so he bids $170,000. Skip decides that's good enough—he almost sold for $166,000. He sells his share to Bob and moves to Florida.

Auction Bidding

☐ If the partners cannot agree who has the right to purchase the other partners' interest in the business, that right shall be determined by an auction, where each group of partners shall bid on the business. The group eventually offering the highest bid shall have the right to buy the lower bidders' shares of the business. The buying group shall pay for the purchased share of the business under the terms provided in this Agreement.

RELATED TOPIC

Paying the buyout price when there's a conflict. Providing a clause that determines who has the right to buy when partners are in conflict doesn't cover how the prevailing partner will pay the losing partner the buyout price. To accomplish that, you need a specific payment clause. (See "Payments to Departing Partners," below.) And if the prevailing partner is determined by coin flip, you also need a clause to determine the buyout price. (See "Determining the Value of the Business," below.)

Determining the Value of the Business

You need clauses in your partnership agreement to define the terms on which remaining partners can buy out the interest of a departing partner, unless a right of first refusal clause governs. (To remind you, in that case, the price and conditions of the outside would-be buyer's offer controls.) Here we focus on what's usually the most important, and thorniest, subject—valuing the business. Even for a very successful small business, finding an outside buyer who wants to buy a portion of it and will pay a fair price can be difficult, or even impossible. So how do you create a fair method for determining the worth of your business when there's no price determined by an open market?

Even with a file of current financial data, coming up with a fair price for partnership business is not easy. While no method will be perfect, working out one now, when you're setting up your partnership, allows you to discuss and agree on a method when none of you are considering selling out, and when you can all, hopefully, see both sides of the equation.

Below we'll discuss and present sample clauses for valuation approaches that we believe are as good as can be achieved. No one method is inherently superior to others. It all depends on the nature of your business, and the partners' relationship and expectations. So don't just settle on one of the methods we present if none seems to fit your situation. You can modify one, blend two, or come up with your own method altogether. Remember, the goal is to achieve as fair a method as possible of determining a buyout price, and your own ingenuity can be used to the fullest.

We do not provide sophisticated valuation methods individually tailored to your business. Occasionally, a more industry-specific approach might seem to lead to a more accurate estimation of the worth of your business. For the vast majority of small businesses, though, especially beginning ones, such detailed methods merely bog you down in complexities, without leading to fairer results.

If you decide you now want to go beyond the basic methods we provide here, you can explore these routes:

- Consult with an expert, such as an experienced business appraiser or a trusted accountant who has experience with the valuation methods commonly used for your type of business.
- If you know other people in your business, you might also wish to discuss with them how they go about valuing their businesses. There are rough valuation norms based on profits, sales, and cash flow for some types of businesses.

RESOURCE

Want more information on valuing a business? There are several good books that concentrate on business-valuation techniques for small businesses, including *Handbook of Business Valuation*, by Thomas L. West and Jeffrey D. Jones (John Wiley & Sons).

Revising Your Valuation Method

Now your business is just beginning. It is probably worth no more than the resale value of its tangible assets. This means that by adopting a valuation clause now, you're really making your best guess as to how you'll value your (hopefully) profitable business in the future. In that future, you may decide to reevaluate and rewrite this clause, assuming your business has become large and successful enough to warrant a more sophisticated evaluation method.

It's wise to structure your agreement so that the business is given a good chance to survive. If the buyout price is too high, the remaining partners may simply decide to liquidate the business. If they do, and the business can't be sold to outsiders, everyone will likely receive much less than if the existing partners bought out the departing partner and the business continued. For example, if a dog-grooming business dissolves, the money received from the sale of secondhand dog-grooming equipment and other business assets should be much less than what the owners could have earned if they'd continued the business.

Also, when considering valuation methods, take into account how buyout payments will be made (covered below). Often a somewhat higher buyout price may be acceptable to the remaining partners in exchange for reasonable monthly payments (instead of a lump sum). And it's helpful—although often difficult with new businesses—to make some earnings projections and see how a buyout method looks in the context of the amount of cash that's likely to be available. For example, if you're being bought out—or buying—in a couple of years, does what you would receive seem like a fair price if the partnership profits are $50,000 a year? $500,000 a year? What about if the business isn't profitable but it appears it soon will be?

If you are entering a partnership in which the major assets are each partner's customers, and any departing partner will take his or her customers upon leaving, what remains for the other partners to pay for? This is a common problem in some types of service businesses, like architects or hairstylists. Normally, all that needs to be valued here are fixed assets like desks, computers, and chairs.

The Asset Valuation Method

The asset valuation method of valuing a business is based on the current net worth of the business. Basically, under this method, the worth of the business is its assets minus its liabilities. The UPA requires you to use this method if your partnership agreement does not contain any specified valuation method.

Here's how it works: As of the date the departing partner leaves, the net dollar value of all partnership assets is calculated and all outstanding business debts are deducted to determine net worth. The departing partner receives his or her ownership percentage of this amount (under whatever payout terms you've agreed on). The net worth of business assets normally includes the following:

- The current market value of all tangible assets of the business. This includes the net value of current inventory, plus the present value of other items, from manufacturing machinery to the stained glass lamps in the waiting room. You get to decide how picky to be here.

- All accounts receivable that are reasonably collectible.
- All earned but unbilled fees, and all money presently earned for work in progress. (This is particularly important in professional partnerships—an architectural firm, for instance—but it can also apply if construction work is being done, or if money is earned although a bill had not yet been sent out. This, technically, is not an account receivable.)
- All cash. (If there isn't sufficient cash to cover debts, they are subtracted from accounts receivable or earned but unbilled fees.)

EXAMPLE: Lou, Wilbur, and George have been equal partners in a computer repair business for four years. Lou quits. Under their partnership agreement, Lou is entitled to one-third of the value of the repair shop, as determined by the asset valuation method. The value of the assets includes all cash in the bank, fixed assets (such as tools, building, and so on), accounts receivable (money people still owe them for fixing their computers), earned but unbilled fees, and money presently earned for work in progress. These assets are all added up and then any money the business owes (liabilities) is deducted to determine the value of the business.

The asset valuation method can be sensible for new businesses. Aside from your hopes, what does your business really have except its fixed assets? There's no reasonable way to estimate future profits when the business has yet to establish a valuable name or reputation. This method can also make sense for a business whose worth is basically determined by the value of tangible possessions, such as an antique store.

However, for many businesses that have been established and profitable for a while, this method fails to include intangible, but still real, aspects of a business's worth. Some ongoing businesses are often worth much more than the value of assets minus liabilities. We must add that Bernard Kamoroff, author of the well-respected *Small Time Operator* (Taylor Trade Publishing), says that extra worth for most small businesses in Main Street America is a fantasy. Basically, he claims, they sell for the value of inventory and fixtures, period.

EXAMPLE: Suppose the computer repair business we mentioned above has a net worth, under the asset valuation method, of $150,000, including: $46,000 worth of equipment, tools, and office furniture; $82,000 in billed fees owed; $28,000 in earned but unbilled fees; $4,000 cash; minus $10,000 owed on the business's line of credit. But thanks to several very profitable service contracts, profits have averaged $180,000 a year for the past four years. Under the asset valuation method, Lou's interest is worth $50,000— one-third of the total value of $150,000. But the profits he's been earning are $60,000 a year.

When Lou leaves, the remaining two partners won't be able to simply divide up his yearly profits. They'll either have to work harder or hire someone to do Lou's work. Still, Lou's interest in the business seems worth substantially more than $50,000. Wouldn't you be glad to pay $50,000 to earn $60,000 a year?

Some profitable ongoing businesses are undoubtedly worth significantly more than the value of their tangible assets because they've earned a good business reputation. That reputation brings in continued business. This intangible asset is traditionally labeled "goodwill," and is generally defined as "the well-founded expectation of continued public patronage." The concept is especially applicable for successful retail businesses (for example, a restaurant with an excellent location and good reputation) but is often less of a factor with businesses that depend primarily on individual service. A carpenter or podiatrist may have acquired personal goodwill, but it's usually hard to transfer that goodwill to another person.

Beginning businesses don't have goodwill, so it can be sensible to adopt a market value buyout method for the first year (or some other set time), with the express provision that another more inclusive method will be adopted at the end of that period.

If you feel sure that you will want to include goodwill in your business valuation, you can simply add it to the list of assets to be valued. However, if you do, be aware that this just puts off the problem of valuing something that is, by definition, hard to value. If you decide goodwill is, or will soon be, a valuable asset of your business, we advise you to set up a method for calculating that value now, and not to postpone the problem. We discuss goodwill in more depth below. If you think that goodwill may apply to you now, be sure you've read that section carefully before making your final decision on your business valuation clause.

Following are clauses you can use, or adapt, if you decide an asset valuation clause is appropriate for your business.

Asset Valuation Method

☐ Except as otherwise provided in this Agreement, the value of the partnership shall be made by determining the net worth of the partnership as of the date a partner leaves, for any reason. Net worth is defined as the market value, as of that date, of the following assets:

1. All tangible property, real or personal, owned by the business;

2. All the liquid assets owned by the business, including cash on hand, bank deposits and CDs, or other monies;

3. All accounts receivable;

4. All earned but unbilled fees;

5. All money presently earned for work in progress;

6. Less the total amount of all debts owed by the business.

Note that this clause (and all the business valuation clauses in this section) commences with "Except as otherwise provided in this Agreement." The reason for this provision is that most agreements will contain a right of first refusal clause. Under this type of clause, you'll recall, if an outsider makes a bona fide offer to buy a partner's interest, its value is determined by this offer, not by the business valuation clause in the agreement.

When using the asset valuation method, you can provide now that you'll revisit your business valuation clause after a set period, to make sure this method continues to be the best one for you. Of course, you can always amend your valuation clause, no matter what method you use. Because the asset valuation method is so rudimentary, it seems particularly appropriate to specify in your agreement that you'll later check out if you still want to use it.

Following are clauses you can use or adapt to state you'll amend your agreement later to include goodwill. Of course, if you decide later there isn't any goodwill, you're not compelled to revise the agreement.

Revision of Valuation Method

☐ The partners agree that _____ years after the commencement of the business, they will revise this valuation clause so that the method used will best reflect the worth of the business.

Revision of Valuation Method to Include Goodwill

☐ The partners understand and agree that the preceding business valuation clause may not fully and adequately reflect the worth of the business after it has been successfully established, if the business has acquired goodwill or other valuable intangible assets. Therefore, the partners agree that __[time period]__ after the commencement of the business they will meet to consider amending this business valuation clause to include a method that will fairly reflect any goodwill earned by the business.

The Book Value Method

A variation of the asset valuation method is called the "book value" method. This means calculating the value of all partnership assets and liabilities as they're set forth in the partnership accounting books. Basically, assets are valued at their acquisition cost. This method has simplicity to recommend it, but little else. Often, the book value of an asset has little relation to reality. And the book value method does not, of course, cover goodwill. Worse, the acquisition cost of property is unlikely to be its current worth. Some property, particularly real estate, can be worth much more than its acquisition cost. Other property, from inventory to office furniture, is probably worth less than its acquisition cost. These assets may have been depreciated on the books, but even with depreciation, usually taken for tax purposes, the book figure may not be close to what the assets can be sold for. Finally, significant assets, such as earned but unbilled fees and money earned for work in progress, aren't included at all.

Because we believe this method is undesirable for almost all businesses, we do not provide a clause for it. We mention it only because we know it has a catchy name ("Hey, doesn't 'book value' make sense?"). There's something about the terms "the books" or the "financial books" that can sound more reliable than they are in this context. So we wanted to clear up that book value isn't a sensible way to go.

Using Capital Accounts as the Basis for Valuation

The term "capital account" means, at its most basic, the amount a partner has invested in the partnership business, less any capital distributions. You may wonder if you could use the dollar figure in each partner's capital account to determine the dollar value of that partner's interest for buyout purposes. The answer is that this is not a good idea. The value of a partner's interest depends on how the business is doing, not on how much he or she invested. After all, investing means you are taking a risk. If the business is doing poorly, it could, at the time a partner leaves, be worth far less than the sum of all the partners' capital accounts. So you don't want to guarantee that departing partners will automatically get back all that they have invested. By contrast, if the business has become very successful, it could be worth far more than the sum of the capital accounts.

The Set-Dollar Method

Under the set-dollar method, the partners agree in advance that if one partner leaves the partnership, the others will buy out his or her share at a predetermined price. Assigning a value to the business has the advantage of being definite, but otherwise can have serious drawbacks. Why? First, because the price selected may be arbitrary and not related to the real current value. Second, because the worth of any partnership business will fluctuate, any predetermined buyout figure may soon become out of date. One way to handle this second problem is to require that the partners establish a value for the partnership every year by a specified date.

A set-dollar figure can be advisable if the primary worth of the business is the energies of the partners, there is no considerable inventory of goods, and the intangible assets of the business (name, goodwill, and so on) have little independent value. This describes many partnership service businesses, particularly in their first few years. From computer repairs to gardening work, many new service businesses don't have costly fixed assets. What they have is the energies and hopes of their owners. Rather than bother with trying to determine the worth of each item of business property using the asset valuation method (the present value of secondhand computer repair tools or pruning tools, etc.), the partners simply determine what they think the business is worth and revise this figure periodically. After all, who knows their business better than they do?

It may also make sense to use a set-dollar buyout clause if the partners' main concern is the preservation of the business and their relationship with each other. For example, we know of a two-man partnership that runs a trucking firm. Neither partner has immediate family to inherit his interest in the firm and both want to ensure the business survives the death of a partner. So they selected what they thought was a low set-dollar estimate for the worth of the business, to be used in the event either partner died. Because the value is set in advance, the deceased partner's estate has no role in valuing the partnership interest. And, because this amount is reasonably low, the survivor should not be unduly burdened to come up with the money.

Another situation where the set-dollar method can make sense is when the partnership is involved in property investment. The partners hope the property will increase in value, although the amount, of course, can't be predicted. (If it could, we'd all get rich.) A prime example of this is investing in real estate. Rather than bother with annual appraisals by professionals, which can be costly and time-consuming—and result in surprising discrepancies between one expert's appraisal price and another's—the partners simply meet yearly and decide what they believe the partnership property is worth. Because real estate is bought and sold on an open market, the partners simply make a sensible estimation of the property's worth based on recent sales of comparable property.

If partners want to be very thorough, they can also agree on the amount or percentage rate they estimate the value of the partnership will increase or decrease over the next year. Thus, if a partner leaves six months after the last yearly valuation, they have a formula for business valuation, which includes recent price fluctuation.

The attraction of the set-dollar method for many partnerships is that it combines fairness and simplicity. The buyout price is fair because everyone has agreed to it. Once you and your partners have determined the price, you don't need to bother with appraisals, accountants, or multipliers if a partner leaves. In effect, the set-dollar method acknowledges that valuing a small business partnership that can't readily be sold on a market is inherently subjective. So the partners face that subjectivity themselves, directly, rather than look to some other valuation method to cope with it. Using the set-dollar method requires the partners to sit down regularly and work out the business's worth, which can help keep all partners up to date on valuation issues and quite possibly defuse potential disputes.

Set-Dollar Method

☐ Except as otherwise provided in this Agreement, the value of a partner's interest in the partnership shall be determined as follows:

1. Within ___[specify, for example, 90]___ days after the end of each fiscal year of the partnership, the partners shall determine the partnership's value by unanimous written agreement, and that value shall remain in effect from the date of that written determination until the next such written determination.

2. Should the partners be unable to agree on a value or otherwise fail to make any such determination, the partnership's value shall be the greater of (a) the value last established under this section, or (b) _[whatever else you decide upon, such as "the net worth of the partnership"]_ .

3. _[Add any further provision you've agreed on, such as that you'll also make annual estimates of the rate of increase or decrease of the value of the business.]_

Postdeparture Appraisal

Using this method, you simply agree to have an independent appraiser (sometimes named in the agreement) determine the value of the partnership at the date of a partner's departure. At first glance, this sounds great. "Hey, why struggle with valuation now? Let an expert determine the precise value later if we ever need to." Sadly, appraisals rarely work so easily. Many small businesses aren't amenable to precise valuation, no matter how expert the appraiser. For most small businesses, all you're doing is passing the buck and hoping that somehow the word "expert" means that a tough problem will be competently solved by someone else.

Even in an area where there is an open market that should allow prices to be determined "objectively," the variation in appraisals can be disturbing.

There are several other reasons to be cautious about using appraisers to determine the value of your business. It can take some time to get the appraiser's report, unless you have the good fortune of finding an appraiser who is both experienced in your business and prompt. Also, the appraisal method (unlike the other methods we discuss) makes it difficult to determine in advance what a partnership interest might be worth. This could mean partners don't have essential information when they need it, as would be the case for someone contemplating leaving a partnership. Also, appraisals aren't cheap, and can be an added cost just when you're worrying about money most.

Having presented the possible drawbacks to the appraisal method, let us now give the other side. Because no valuation method is precise or scientific, appraisal can, in some situations, be the best of your difficult choices. Some businesses are more suitable to valuation by appraisal than others. Any business where there is a closely followed market that can be used to determine the price of inventory can sensibly use the appraisal method.

Beyond this, the key to making the appraisal method work is to agree ahead of time on an appraiser all partners have confidence in. For example, if you and your partners are starting a small software business, you would want to appoint someone of unquestioned integrity and judgment who knows the software industry—preferably, your segment of it—intimately.

Below is a clause for the appraisal valuation method. While it's possible to set out criteria the appraiser must use or consider in making an appraisal of your business, we don't think this is wise. If the appraiser is inexperienced or unskilled, no amount of detail in your agreement will make the appraisal more trustworthy. And, if the appraiser knows what he or she is doing, your criteria are likely to be restrictive rather than helpful.

Postdeparture Appraisal

☐ Except as otherwise provided in this Agreement, the value of the partnership shall be determined by an independent appraisal conducted, if possible, by ___*[name of agreed-on person]*___ . If all partners cannot agree on an appraiser, the departing partner and the remaining partners shall each select an independent appraiser. If the two selected appraisers are unable to agree on the fair market value of the partnership business, then the two appraisers shall mutually select a third appraiser to determine the fair market value.

The appraisal shall be commenced within _____ days of the partner's departure from the partnership. The partnership and the departing partner shall share the cost of the appraisal equally.

The Capitalization-of-Earnings Method

"Capitalization of earnings" is a fancy term for a method that determines the value of a business based on what it makes. Often, the best estimate of what a business is really worth (without an open market to set the price) depends in large measure on its earning capacity. If the business is successful and likely to remain so even if a partner leaves, the capitalization-of-earnings method accounts for the real value in the ongoing nature of the successful business. For example, take two restaurants that are each worth $150,000 according to the asset valuation method, but one has yearly profits of $250,000 and the other has yearly profits of $30,000. Clearly, the more successful restaurant is really worth much more than the other. As we've discussed, this is commonly referred to as a business having "goodwill." Other intangible assets can range from a desirable lease to valuable intellectual property, including patents, copyrights, and trade names. The capitalization-of-earnings method is an attempt to include these intangible assets when determining the worth of a business.

The theory of the capitalization-of-earnings method is simple:

1. You determine what the business earns (usually on a yearly basis) over a set period of years.
2. You multiply this earnings figure by a predetermined number, the "multiplier."

EXAMPLE: The four partners of Ace Furniture planned their business well. They obtained a low-rent 30-year lease on their store. Now, after five years in business, that store is, as they thought it would be, in the center of a rapidly gentrifying city neighborhood. The partners are astute selectors of furniture their customers want. Sales are good and profits have averaged $213,000 per year the past two years. One partner decides to leave. The partners have decided the value of the business is two times the average net profits for the past two years. The buyout price is $426,000.

If you're just starting your partnership, or the partnership hasn't been in existence very long when a partner leaves, it's premature to value your business by the capitalization-of-earnings method. With this method, you usually select a base period of two to five years. If you look at just one year, you might end up choosing a particularly good, or bad, year. Therefore, you may want to adopt another valuation provision for your first years and then switch over to the capitalization-of-earnings method later. But it's not premature for you to explore the capitalization-of-earnings method now, when your business is just beginning. If you plan or hope to switch to this method in a few years, all partners should understand now how the method they want to use in the future will work.

Suppose your business has been profitable for several years. Does the capitalization-of-earnings method necessarily make sense? Not automatically. You must first be sure the business has goodwill.

Once you've determined that your business really has acquired goodwill or has other valuable intangible assets, you then can sensibly use the capitalization-of-earnings method to determine its value. There's no one set of criteria that exclusively determines how the capitalization-of-earnings method works. Rather, there are four basic factors involved:

1. What earnings are measured—gross income or net profits?
2. What period of time are earnings measured (averaged) over?
3. What multiplier is used to multiply average earnings to determine the capitalized earnings?
4. Are any other items, such as the value of fixed assets, also included in the valuation?

Let's look at each item individually.

The Measure of Earnings

The simplest way to state the issue here is: net or gross? At first blush, it seems that net earnings make the most sense, because they show what matters for buyout purposes. After all, a business with a substantial gross income but no net earnings isn't worth much, is it? Well, maybe it is. Accounting figures don't always reflect financial reality. You need to know whether the business earns what is called undisclosed income. Especially in cash businesses, it's not unusual for an occasional sum— sometimes $20, and other times much more—to disappear into the owners' pockets, never making it to the books. Also, many businesses that honestly report all their income still find legal, if sometimes inventive, ways to consume that income as business expenses, leaving little or no net earnings. In addition, most small businesses can fairly easily inflate or deflate earnings by decisions to hire, expand, buy equipment, and the like.

For these reasons, some experienced partnership lawyers often use gross income as the base figure for the capitalization-of-earnings method. Our preference is still to use net earnings—but if you do, be sure they are fairly calculated.

The Time Period

Using this method, you'll want to use the base of the earnings, or profits, of your business over a number of years, not simply one. A longer time period is less apt to be skewed by erratic short-term economic fluctuations. There's no set magic figure for the number of years. Sometimes partners agree to the last three years, or five, or seven—whatever gives them security that the long haul has been taken into account.

The Multiplier

The multiplier is the number by which the earnings, however you've defined them, are multiplied to determine the value of the business. Where does the multiplier come from? Hopefully, not out of thin air. It's not easy, though, to agree on a multiplier that will produce a fair result. No outsider can definitively say what a fair multiplier is for you. The best advice we can give you is to pick various numbers and make projections. Do any of them seem to give a fair buyout price?

An experienced, cautious partnership adviser we know says he believes the multiplier should never be higher than three; anything more is likely to cripple a small business.

In some industries, there are somewhat established norms that help provide the multiplier. Construction companies, retail stores, and restaurants are examples of businesses where there are conventional multiple norms. You can obtain standard multipliers for these and various other industries from business evaluators or brokers who specialize in a particular industry.

You shouldn't accept these norms without plenty of caution, however. The general economy or a particular local economy that affects your business can change so quickly that last year's multipliers can become irrelevant this year. In addition, remember that no two businesses are the same. Two auto repair shops that earn $200,000 each may be headed in opposite directions.

If you use a multiplier based on gross earnings rather than profits, you will want to think in terms of a fraction (for example, in a fairly profitable business, one-third of gross earnings).

Other Factors Included in the Buyout Price

Partners can decide that they want the buyout price to be a combination of capitalization of earnings and other factors, such as the current net value of fixed assets or the amount in each partner's capital account. Again, there are no ironclad rules. Just make sure your method doesn't set the buyout price so high that no one can pay it, or the business will die if a partner leaves.

If you want to use a capitalization-of-earnings method to determine buyout price, here's a clause you can use or adapt:

The Capitalization-of-Earnings Method

☐ Except as otherwise provided in this Agreement, the value of the partnership shall be determined as follows:

1. The average yearly earnings of the business shall be calculated for the preceding _[define this period]_ ;

2. "Earnings," as used in this clause, is defined as: _[define, such as "net earnings: annual gross revenue minus annual expenses and all taxes" or "gross income"]_ ;

3. The average yearly earnings shall then be multiplied by a multiple of _____ to give the value of the business, except as provided for in Section 4, below;

4. [_If you want to include additional factors in the buyout price, do so here; such as "the value of fixed assets minus liabilities."_]

_____

_____.

Varying the Buyout Price

There's one additional factor that you may want to consider regarding determining a buyout price. Does it make a difference why or when a partner departs? Many partnerships have decided it does. How long you've been in business when a partner leaves may also be a factor. For example, a partner who leaves during the initial stage of a business (whatever time period you pick; partners often choose one or two years), may be entitled only to the book value of his or her interest. After this initial period, a departing partner's interest is calculated by a method that more accurately reflects the current operation and success of the business.

Also, some partnerships adopt different prices (or different methods for calculating the price) for a departing partner's interest, depending on the reason the partner leaves. For example, in a professional partnership of architects we know, the buyout provision varies considerably, depending on whether the departing architect:

- becomes disabled, retires over age 65, or dies (this is the highest buyout provision, partially because insurance can cover much of the cost)
- quits to pursue some other nonarchitectural dream (for example, moves to Tahiti or becomes a full-time flute player), or
- quits, but remains an architect. (This results in the lowest buyout provision, because it assumes that some of the architect's clients would likely stick with him. If the departing partner remains active as an architect in the same county as his former partnership, the buyout provision is even lower.)

Another reason to vary the buyout price is a partner's failure to give the required advance notice, as discussed earlier. Some partnerships decide to impose a severe sanction here, making the price, say, one-half what it otherwise would be; others are far more lenient. And many ignore this problem altogether.

There are no set rules we can give you regarding varying your buyout clause. You really need to create your own solutions here. Discuss this question carefully. Then write down your own decisions.

Variation of the Buyout Price

☐ The preceding method for calculating the value of the business shall be varied as stated below, for the reasons stated below:

_____

_____.

Using Insurance to Value a Partner's Interest

A business or another partner can buy life or disability insurance on each partner. You can then state in your agreement that the money the policy pays to the estate of a deceased partner, or to a disabled partner, shall be the full worth of that partner's interest in the partnership. This makes valuation very easy for disabled or deceased partners' interests—you do it when you decide what policy to buy or keep.

Insurance Proceeds: Disability or Death of a Partner

☐ If a partner becomes disabled, or dies, the value of his or her interest in the partnership, including for estate purposes, shall be the proceeds paid by the disability or death insurance policy maintained by the partnership, or the other partners, for that partner.

Other Valuation Issues

As we've said, there are many possible valuation methods. If you come up with one that is different from those we suggest, fine. Write it up and put it in your agreement. Don't worry about putting it in legalese; clear English will suffice. Some partners base the valuation on some simple formula that they find to be practical and is agreed upon by all the partners.

Divorce

A spouse may have a legal interest in a partnership entered into by the other spouse. This is generally true in community property states (Alaska and Tennessee (by spousal agreement), Arizona, California, Idaho, Nevada, New Mexico, Texas, Washington, and Wisconsin), where each spouse owns one-half of all community property. It may also be true in common law states, especially at divorce, where equitable distribution laws require that marital property be divided fairly. If both spouses have legal interests in a partnership and there's a divorce, the partnership may well have to be appraised or evaluated for divorce settlement purposes. Many partnerships understandably don't want the valuation clause they've carefully prepared to be ignored in a divorce proceeding. The best way to try to prevent this is to have all spouses sign the partnership agreement, too. Often at the end of the agreement, by the partners' signature clause, there's an additional clause for spouses.

> CAUTION
>
> **Be sure your spouse understands what he or she is signing.** If you want spouses to approve the partnership agreement and sign it, be sure that each spouse genuinely understands what's in the agreement, and what he or she is consenting to. Don't just hand them a document and say something like, "Here, dear, sign this." The goal is not, obviously, to sneak something past your spouse. Aside from the weird karma involved in trying that, you could wind up with a spousal consent that would be struck down by a court in any subsequent divorce proceeding.

Here's a clause you can use or adapt so spouses agree to the terms of your partnership agreement.

Consent of Spouse

☐ I, ___[name]___ , the [husband/wife] of ___[partner's name]___ , have read and understand this Partnership Agreement and hereby consent to all clauses and terms in it. I specifically agree that the business valuation method contained in the Agreement shall be used in any legal proceeding to determine the value of any interest I may have in the business.

___[signature of spouse]___

[dated]

> ! CAUTION
>
> **Be sure to obtain a consent of a spouse if one of the partners gets married after you've signed your partnership agreement.** Once you've created your agreement, it's easy to stick it in a drawer and forget about it. But when one partner goes through a major life event, such as getting married, it's worth taking it out and looking at it to make sure your agreement still meets every partner's needs.

Estate Taxes

One additional possible benefit of buyout clauses involves estate taxes. If the estate of a deceased partner will be subject to federal estate taxes, it can be useful to have a valuation method for his or her interest in the partnership agreement.

Under the current law, very few deceased partners' estates will be subject to estate tax. During 2020, federal law exempts $11,580,000 per individual from estate tax. The federal estate tax is indexed for inflation on a yearly basis. So the amount of the exemption will increase for 2021 and thereafter, unless the United States suddenly suffers from deflation, which seems unlikely.

In additional to federal estate taxes, a few states impose state estate or inheritance taxes.

If a deceased partner's estate must pay estate tax, the value of his or her partnership interest must be independently evaluated, unless there's a reasonable valuation clause in the partnership agreement. Often, an independent estate tax evaluation produces a higher figure for the worth of a business than the worth determined under a valuation clause. If there is a valuation clause, the IRS will normally accept what you say your deceased partner's share is worth, as long as the clause contains the following provisions:

- The people who inherit part of the business are obligated to sell it.
- The remaining partners are obligated to purchase the business interest of their dead partner, or at least have an option to purchase it.
- The partnership agreement forbids partners from disposing of their interest during their lifetimes without first offering it to the other partners.
- The agreement is the result of an arm's length transaction; that is, it cannot be a (disguised) gift.

Tax Consequences of a Majority Partner Selling Out

Under federal law (Internal Revenue Code Section 708(a)), a partnership is terminated for U.S. income tax purposes if either of the following apply:

- No part of the business is carried on by any partner.
- Fifty percent or more of the business (both partnership capital and profits) is sold or transferred within 12 months.

If the partnership is terminated, there can be serious adverse tax consequences for all concerned. All partnership property is considered distributed to the partners and is subject to tax, even if the remaining partners want to continue the business. There are special rules for 50-50 partnerships that prevent the application of the standard tax rules here. (See Chapter 8.) If any partner will own 50% or more of the partnership business, you should consult an accountant or a tax lawyer with partnership tax expertise to minimize the possibility of a formal termination of the partnership.

Some Words of Encouragement

By now, all these different considerations and options regarding buyouts and business valuations may seem overwhelming. You may well be at the stage where you're ready to ask yourself whether you really want to bother with all of this. Or should you just hire a lawyer to do it for you? The answers are—yes and no. When the time comes to buy out a departing partner's interest, you'll be glad you took the time to resolve how to calculate the value of that interest in advance. As any partnership lawyer can assure you, time and time again disputes over the value of a departing partner's interest lead to lawsuits and bitterness. Turning the whole problem over to a lawyer won't solve the problem either. Sure, your lawyer could say, "Okay, here's the method you should use." But a good lawyer won't be so authoritarian. Instead, he or she will tell you to puzzle over the same issues and possible solutions we discuss here and arrive at the substance of what you think is fair. It's your business, and no one else should decide how you determine what it's worth. This doesn't mean that you shouldn't consult a lawyer, only that you should, at the very least, understand what's involved before you do.

Payments to Departing Partners

How does a departing partner get paid? In a lump sum, or over time? If the payments are over time, for how long a time? These issues are closely related to which method you choose for determining the buyout price. Think of it this way: If the remaining partners can pay over a number of years, they are usually willing to pay a higher buyout price than if they must come up with the whole amount right after a partner leaves.

Determining the Payment Schedule

It's essential to decide on a buyout payment schedule. A lump sum payment is rarely advisable. However, if you fail to adopt a payment schedule, the UPA provides, in essence, that the departing partner has the right to collect the full amount promptly. This can become a serious problem, especially in the event of a partner's death, because the deceased partner's estate and inheritors will likely insist on exercising this right.

> **EXAMPLE:** Eric and Jack went into partnership to build a house they intended to rent. In the building stage, they became intimate friends, and the house ended up their single family home. Some years later, Eric dies suddenly, and leaves his share of the house to his daughter. Eric's daughter demands full payment of Eric's share immediately. Because there is no payment schedule in Jack's and Eric's agreement, and Jack can't raise half the value of the house immediately, he has no choice but to sell the house he built and now lives in.

Paying off a departing or deceased partner's share all at once often requires the partnership to sell important partnership assets, which may: (1) destroy the business; and (2) bring in much less than the full value of the sold assets because you had to resort to a hurried distress sale.

It makes good business sense to adopt a payment method that puts a premium on the survival of the business. If the payment terms are so severe that the business can't afford them, everyone will lose. And even if the terms wouldn't necessarily end the business, the remaining owners may still decide to liquidate the partnership business and go on to other things. In ending a partnership—as in starting and running one—the best approach is to have the partners share the benefits fairly. On the other hand, the partner leaving (or his or her inheritors, if there's a death) has a real interest in getting money reasonably fast. No one wants to be hostage to someone else's business judgment for years to come. If the surviving partners make bad choices, it could wipe out money that really should go to the departing partner. This can be a particularly intense concern if the departing partner is pulling out precisely because of a lack of trust. You have to balance these competing and conflicting concerns to arrive at what you think are fair payment terms.

You can adopt any installment payment schedule that fits your needs. You could agree to pay a fixed sum, or a set percentage of the total price, and then make payments each month or quarter or year. It's also possible to provide for payments to increase or decrease over a set number of years, or payments with interest added or not. You could obtain a bank loan to pay off the departing partner, then pay the bank in installments. This method, obviously, requires that the business be able to obtain a substantial loan, and that the remaining partners accept the added obligation of loan interest.

Once again, there's no simple, set formula. You have to create a method for payment that suits your business and your temperaments. Many partnerships decide not to extend payments over more than two to five years. (This may seem to be a short period of time to raise all the money you'll need, but remember that if the business is prospering, you'll be able to borrow from a bank or, if necessary, you can find a new partner with capital to contribute.) A common provision is to delay the first payment for some set time, such as 90 days, in order to give the remaining partners time to start gathering the funds.

We want to remind you that as with your buy-sell clause, you're not required to stick with your payment clause when a partner leaves if none of you wants to. Again, you're creating a floor, not a ceiling—this is simply the method you'll use if you don't all agree on another one later. For instance, suppose your partnership agreement calls for a five-year payment plan, with interest at 10% per year on the unpaid balance. Now suppose seven years later, when your business is prosperous, a departing partner says, "You know, I'd like to get as much cash as I can now. If you all agree, you can give me, right now, 60% of what I would have received over five years." Obviously, if this seems fair to the remaining partners, they can substitute it for the five-year payment plan.

> ⓘ CAUTION
>
> **If you vary the terms of the partnership agreement, put it in writing.**
> Just as it makes sense to draft a written amendment if you permanently change part of your partnership agreement, you should document any major, one-time deviations from its terms. That way, there's less of a chance that the partners will be confused or (heaven forbid) try to claim that they didn't agree to the change.

Here's a clause providing for equal monthly installment payments:

Equal Monthly Payments

☐ Whenever the partnership is obligated or chooses to purchase a partner's interest in the partnership, it shall pay for that interest by promissory note of the partnership. Any promissory note shall be dated as of the effective date of the purchase, shall mature in not more than _____ years, shall be payable in equal installments that come due monthly *[and shall bear interest at the rate of XX % per annum] [and may, at the partnership's option, be subordinated to existing and future debts to banks and other institutional lenders for money borrowed]*. The first payment shall be made _____ days after the date of the promissory note.

Some partnerships agree that a departing partner will be entitled to receive a set sum as part of the buyout price upon leaving or shortly after leaving the partnership. The partner then gets payments of the balance due over time. This set sum can be a fixed dollar amount or, more commonly, a percentage of the overall buyout figure.

If you decide on this approach, here's a clause you can use.

Lump Sum, Then Equal Monthly Payments

☐ Whenever the partnership is obligated or chooses to purchase a partner's interest in the partnership, it shall pay for that interest as follows:

First: It shall pay the departing partner _[define lump sum payment]_ within _[time allowed]_ . Second: After that initial payment, it shall pay the balance owed by promissory note of the partnership. Any promissory note shall be dated as of the effective date of the purchase, shall mature in not more than _____ years, shall be payable in equal installments that come due monthly [_and shall bear interest at the rate of XX % per annum_] [_and may, at the partnership's option, be subordinated to existing and future debts to banks and other institutional lenders for money borrowed_]. The first payment shall be made ____ days after the date of the promissory note.

Although we do not recommend using it, we provide here a clause for full cash payment, within a relatively short time after a partner leaves the business.

Cash Payment

☐ Whenever the partnership is obligated or chooses to purchase a partner's interest in the partnership, it shall pay for that interest in cash, within _[whatever time period you choose]_ .

The Departing Partner's Responsibility for Partnership Debts

A departing partner is legally responsible for all outstanding debts and obligations of the partnership incurred up to the date he or she leaves. No agreement between the partnership and the departing partner can alter this liability to outside creditors. However, as part of a buyout clause, the partnership can expressly assume the obligation to pay all debts of the firm, including any share owed by the departing partner. This type of clause won't protect a departing partner if the business goes broke, especially if the other partners are broke, too. But if the partnership, or any of the remaining partners, have assets to pay off old debts, the departing partner is protected.

Assumption of Departing Partner's Liabilities

☐ The continuing partnership shall pay, as they come due, all partnership debts and obligations that exist on the date a partner leaves the partnership, and shall hold the departing partner harmless from any claim arising from these debts and obligations.

It's not unusual for the departure of one partner to coincide with the admission of a new one. An incoming partner can also assume full responsibility for the old partner's share of partnership debts. The new partner, however, is under no obligation to do so. And even if the new partner does assume responsibility for the debts and gives a written release to the old partner, this doesn't automatically leave that old partner completely in the clear. (See Chapter 4 for more information.)

Expelling a Partner

It's quite unusual for a small business partnership to expel a partner. We know of many partnerships that have dissolved completely, and some in which, say, two partners remain and one leaves, but formal expulsions are very rare. Perhaps this is because many partners in small businesses decide not to cover possible expulsion in a separate clause. They reason that because everything they decide and do must be unanimous, if they ever reach the stage where they're considering an expulsion, it's time to disband the partnership. This can make sense for very small partnerships. It doesn't for larger partnerships, where it's usually not practical to end the business just because one partner is impossible to deal with. Even though it may never be used, large partnerships should include an expulsion clause in their partnership agreement.

Courts hesitate to enforce expulsion clauses if there is room for ambiguity or doubt. For example, courts are reluctant to expel a partner, or enter a decree of dissolution of a partnership, based on the mental or bodily health of that partner. If it's important to you that all partners be healthy, or nonsmokers, and you want them out if they're not, say so clearly and set up some sort of criteria by which the partners can make a determination. This same sort of clarity should be the hallmark of an expulsion clause. Can a simple majority expel a partner? Do there have to be grounds justifying the expulsion? Or do you want a clause that simply says a partner may be expelled for reasons that appear to be sufficient to the other partners?

Below is a sample expulsion clause you can use or adapt. It provides that an expelled partner receives the same payment for his or her interest as a partner who leaves for any other reason. By doing this, you treat the partner who is expelled the same way you treat a partner who leaves for a neutral reason and probably lower the level of bitterness that is likely to surround an expulsion.

Expulsion of a Partner

☐ A partner may be expelled from the partnership by a vote of _[specify vote, such as "three-fourths of the voting partners" or "the other partners holding at least 60% of the capital in the partnership," or whatever you choose]_ .

[Here, you can also add any specific grounds for expulsion that you've agreed on.

_____

_____

_____.]

Expulsion shall become effective when written notice of expulsion is served on the expelled partner. When the expulsion becomes effective, the expelled partner's right to participate in the partnership's profits and his or her other rights, powers, and authority as a partner of the partnership shall terminate. An expelled partner shall be entitled to receive the value of his or her interest in the partnership, as that value is defined in this Agreement.

Bankruptcy and Expulsion

Under the UPA, a partner's personal bankruptcy causes dissolution of a partnership, even if the business itself is still viable. In any partnership, and especially a large one, it can be appropriate to have a provision planning for immediate expulsion of a bankrupt partner. The following clause contains the technical language defining acts constituting bankruptcy and authorizes expulsion for a partner's bankruptcy. (Bankruptcy has its own rules, concepts, and language. Few of you are likely to need to know about all this. If you do, we recommend the books *How to File for Chapter 7 Bankruptcy,* by Albin Renauer and Cara O'Neill (Nolo), and *The New Bankruptcy: Will It Work for You?* by Cara O'Neill (Nolo).)

A Partner's Bankruptcy and Expulsion

☐ Notwithstanding any other provisions of this Agreement, a partner shall cease to be a partner and shall have no interest in common with the remaining partners or in partnership property when the partner does any of the following:

1. Obtains or becomes subject to an order of relief under the Bankruptcy Code.

2. Obtains or becomes subject to an order or decree of insolvency under state law.

3. Makes an assignment for the benefit of creditors.

4. Consents to or accepts the appointment of a receiver or trustee to any substantial part of his or her assets that is not vacated within _____ days.

5. Consents to or accepts an attachment or execution of any substantial part of his or her assets that is not released within _____ days.

From the date of any of the preceding events, he or she shall be considered as a seller to the partnership of his or her interest in the partnership as set forth in this Agreement.

If a partner is expelled for one of the above reasons, the partnership shall not be dissolved, but shall continue to function without interruption.

Arbitration

Expulsions are one area where you may not want to allow the possibility of arbitration. It can be wiser to prohibit any risk that an arbitrator will decide you can't expel a partner after you said you did. So, if you have an arbitration clause in your contract, as we urge (see Chapter 6), you may want to make clear that it doesn't apply to expulsions, and that any expulsion decision is final. There can be a slight risk in this approach, though. A court may be more likely to examine an expulsion decision subject to no other review than it would be if the expulsion were subject to arbitration.

If you want to do the best you can to eliminate review of an expulsion decision, use or adapt the following clause.

Expulsion and Arbitration

☐ Any decision of expulsion made by the partners pursuant to this Agreement shall be final and shall not be subject to arbitration or other review, including review by any court.

As you'll see in Chapter 6, our arbitration clause starts with the phrase "Except as otherwise provided in this Agreement." Thus, the above clause is expressly exempted from the general arbitration clause.

Continuing the Partnership

If a partnership has more than two members, the remaining partners often—indeed, usually—want to continue the business, uninterrupted, when a partner leaves. (If there is only one partner left, he or she may desire to continue the business, but by definition it won't continue as a partnership.) Partners who want to continue to operate the business in the partnership form certainly do not want, or need, a formal dissolution and winding up of the old partnership. Indeed, whatever eventually happens to a partnership business, it's undesirable to wind up the old partnership soon after a partner leaves.

If the business is to continue as a partnership, a technical, formal dissolution of the old one can lead to unpleasant tax consequences. This can include the IRS regarding (old) partnership property as distributed to partners and therefore subject to tax. Even if the business will eventually be disbanded and sold, all interested persons (including the inheritors of a deceased partner) probably want the business to continue at least long enough so that it can be sold in an orderly fashion and not at a fire sale price.

To provide that your partnership continues after a partner leaves, use the following clause:

Partnership Continues

☐ In the case of a partner's death, permanent disability, retirement, voluntary withdrawal, or expulsion from the partnership, the partnership shall not dissolve or terminate, but its business shall continue without interruption and without any break in continuity. On the disability, retirement, withdrawal, expulsion, or death of any partner, the others shall not liquidate or wind up the affairs of the partnership, but shall continue to conduct a partnership under the terms of this Agreement.

Protections Against a Departing Partner

Many business partners decide they want to prohibit a departing or expelled partner from directly competing against the partnership. As many business partners have learned from painful experience, even a partner who leaves under friendly circumstances can easily start up a competing business and drain away a good deal of income from the partnership. You and your partners should decide now what a departing partner may (and may not) do upon leaving the partnership.

A noncompetition clause prevents a departing partner from competing against the partnership for a specified period of time within a specific geographic area after leaving the partnership. Including this clause in your partnership agreement can help protect your trade secrets, as well as your client and customer lists.

While forbidding a partner from engaging in his or her usual way of earning a living is obviously a drastic act, properly drafted noncompetition agreements, especially in the context of a departing partner, are legal in most states. To be legal, a noncompetition agreement must be reasonably limited in both time and geographical area, and be otherwise fair (that is, seem reasonable to a judge under the circumstances). For instance, an agreement that says a partner who voluntarily withdrew from a doughnut shop couldn't open up a competing business within one mile for a period of two years would probably be enforceable, but one that said he could not run a doughnut shop within 100 miles for ten years would almost certainly be thrown out by a judge.

While including this clause in your agreement might seem rather unfair to the departing partner, in some cases it may be warranted. For example, if a partner is taught some unique skill upon admission to the partnership (for example, rebuilding fireplaces or retrofitting houses to withstand earthquakes) and the local area cannot support another enterprise selling that skill, a noncompetition agreement may be fair. By contrast, if the ex-partner has a general skill and no other way to make a living, a noncompetition clause might be struck down by a court. Note that because any noncompetition agreement must be reasonably limited in geographic scope to be legal, the worst that can happen is that the departing partner must run his or her business in another community.

Noncompetition Clause

☐ On the voluntary withdrawal, permanent disability, retirement, or expulsion of any partner, that partner shall not carry on a business the same as or similar to the business of the partnership within the _[describe geographic area]_ for a period of _[time period you've agreed on]_ .

SEE AN EXPERT

Noncompetition law varies in all 50 states. Whatever the specifics of your state's laws, these clauses are not favored by most judges. In legalese, noncompetition clauses are "strictly construed" (against the partnership) by a court. So, if this sort of clause is important to you, we advise you to see a lawyer in your area or do some of your own legal research to make sure your noncompetition clause will hold up in court.

Control of the Business Name

In some businesses, the right to use a name has great value—a famous rock band's name is one obvious example. At the other extreme, Joe & Al's TV Repairs is unlikely to be more valuable than Joe's TV Repairs. If your business name could matter, you should decide who owns it and gets to keep it if someone leaves the partnership. If there are several partners, the usual solution is to let the ongoing partnership retain ownership of that name. However, if yours is an equal-number partnership, you could face trouble with this situation; there could be no majority. Also, it may be that one partner coined the name and wants to be entitled to use it if he or she leaves the partnership or the business ends. And suppose the business uses one person's name—for example, The Toni Ihara Band—and Toni decides to leave the band. It can also happen that one ex-partner doesn't want the name of the former business used at all.

Following are four sample clauses defining who owns your business name if a partner leaves or the business dissolves.

Partnership Continues to Own Name

☐ The partnership business name of _____ is owned by the partnership. Should any partner cease to be a member of the partnership, the partnership shall continue to retain exclusive ownership and right to use the partnership business name.

One Partner Owns Name

☐ The partnership business name of _____ shall be solely owned by ___[person's name]___ if _[he/she]_ ceases to be a partner.

Control of Name to Be Decided at Later Date

☐ The partnership business name of _____ is owned by the partnership. Should any partner cease to be a partner, and desire to use the partnership business name, and the remaining partners desire to continue the partnership and continue use of the partnership business name, ownership and control of the name shall be decided _[insert any method you choose, such a flipping a coin, arbitration, etc.]_ .

Dissolution: Majority Owns Name

☐ In the event of dissolution, the partnership business name of _____ shall be owned by a majority of the former partners. Any other former partner is not entitled to ownership or use of the partnership business name.

The business name may not be the only partnership asset you want to determine ownership of in advance. You can adapt the above clauses to cover copyrights, patents, and trademarks, as well as your business telephone number, licenses, permits, and similar assets.

Insurance and Partners' Estate Planning

Just because there's a provision in a partnership agreement that a departing partner will be paid off on a set schedule doesn't mean the business will actually earn sufficient money to make those payments. Sometimes, making the payments imposes a serious, even grave, drain on cash necessary for other business purposes. So, many partnerships decide to protect themselves to some extent by purchasing insurance against each partner's serious illness, incapacity, or death. (Obviously, these kinds of insurance don't help you pay off a partner who quits or who is expelled.)

For many partnerships, life insurance can be a sensible way of obtaining the money needed to pay off a deceased partner's interest, especially by purchasing term insurance, the cheapest form of life insurance. If a partner dies, the partnership-financed insurance policy pays off his or her share, not partnership operating income.

If you do decide to go the life insurance route, consider solving two problems at once by providing in your partnership agreement that the amount of the life insurance payout is also the value of the deceased partner's interest in the business. You don't have to tie them together this tightly, however. You can use any of the valuation methods discussed above, and then make sure you buy enough life insurance to make any necessary payment if a partner dies.

Here are some useful points about using life insurance policies to finance a buyout agreement:

- Partners have an "insurable interest" in the life of their partners, so they can buy policies on them directly. You can also purchase additional insurance to cover extra costs to the business caused by the death of a partner, such as hiring a new employee.

- There are two different methods of buying life insurance policies: Either the partners buy policies on each other (cross-purchase) or the partnership itself buys the policies. For small partnerships, a cross-purchase plan is usually more desirable. If the partnership itself pays for and owns the policies on the partners, it has been held in some circumstances that the proceeds of the policy are partnership assets and are included in the value of the partnership, thus risking artificially increasing the worth of the deceased partner's share. In a cross-purchase agreement, each partner buys policies on the life of each other partner and this problem is avoided. The following is a provision for the cross-purchase of life insurance:

Cross-Purchase of Life Insurance

☐ Each partner shall purchase and maintain life insurance [and disability insurance] on the life of each other partner in the face value of $ _____.

In a larger partnership, a cross-purchase scheme is usually too cumbersome. If there are six partners, for example, each partner must buy five policies (one on each of the other partners' lives), which means a total of 30 policies. To avoid this much complexity and paperwork, it's probably better to have the partnership pay for a single policy on each partner's life, despite the problem mentioned above. If you do this, specify explicitly that only the cash surrender value of the life insurance policies before the insured's death is a partnership asset, whereas the proceeds themselves are not.

Partnership Insurance Policies

☐ The life insurance policies owned by the partnership on the lives of each partner are assets of the partnership only insofar as they have cash surrender value preceding the death of a partner.

There's also the question of what happens to a life insurance policy if a partner quits or resigns. The usual solution is to allow the departing partner to purchase the policy, since the partnership no longer needs that protection. Here's a clause that covers this:

Insurance Policies and Partner's Departure

☐ On the withdrawal or termination of any partner for any reason other than his or her death [*add* "or disability" *if the partners purchase disability insurance on each other*], any insurance policies on his or her life ["or health"], for which the partnership paid the premiums, shall be delivered to that partner and become his or her separate property. If the policy has a cash surrender value, that amount shall be paid to the partnership by the withdrawing partner, or offset against the partnership's obligations to him or her.

Here are some more facts you should know about life insurance:

- Insurance payments made by a partnership are normally not tax deductible. (Treasury Reg. 1.264-1; unless the policy is a condition for a bank loan with the policy assigned to the bank in case of death.)
- If a partner can't pass a life insurance physical, you have a problem. But unless you think this is reasonably likely, there's little reason to worry about it in the original partnership agreement; solve it when (and if) it arises.
- The partners will eventually want to do some estate planning. This isn't a book about estate planning, but we do want to alert you to the fact that buyout agreements should be coordinated with each partner's individual estate plan. For example, if the proceeds of the insurance policy are payable to the deceased partner's estate, these proceeds are subject to probate and will increase probate fees. In order to avoid probate, someone other than the estate of the deceased partner should be specified as the beneficiary of

each policy. For instance, if a partner intended to leave all her property to her spouse, that spouse could be named as beneficiary of the policy. If the partner has a number of beneficiaries—say her spouse, several children, and some friends—things get a little more complicated, but only a little. For example, by using a living trust, the spouse would name the other spouse, children, and friends as beneficiaries of the trust, to receive the gifts specified in the trust. Then the trust is named as beneficiary of the life insurance policy.

RESOURCE

Want to know more about living trusts? A living trust is a basic probate avoidance device that's normally quite easy to prepare. To create your own living trust, see *Make Your Own Living Trust*, by Denis Clifford, or *Quicken WillMaker &Trust* (software), both by Nolo.

Terminating a Partnership

The legal terms for termination of a partnership business are "winding up" and "dissolution." This means that all partnership business is settled, the partnership books are closed, and the partners go their separate ways. The former partners may continue the former partnership business in some other form, or the business may end altogether.

Do you need to cover termination in your partnership agreement? Not beyond the clauses you'll use from this book to prepare your general agreement. This agreement will handle the basics of your termination— how the business is valued, who gets the business name, and so on. Inevitably, though, there will be other details and fine points to be resolved, matters that haven't been foreseen. Who must cope with the hassle of a supplier pressing for a payment that all partners agree isn't owed? Who gets which customers? The sensible way to handle these details is to talk them over when termination occurs and resolve them between yourselves. Then, prepare a separate termination agreement apart from, and in addition to, the provision in your original partnership agreement.

The Process of Termination

Once the decision has been made to end the partnership, existing partnership business should be completed as speedily as possible. Legally, ending a partnership business involves three stages:

1. First is the dissolution of the partnership—the decision to actually end it. Legally, no new partnership business can be undertaken after this time. If a partner is worried that another partner won't honor this rule, the worried partner can send formal written notices to business contacts that the partnership has been dissolved and cannot undertake new business. (See the sample letter, below.) There is no official or government office where you must record notice that the partnership has dissolved. You can record such a notice at your local county recorder's office, for whatever protection that can provide. (Not much.)

2. Next is winding up the existing partnership business. Partners in a dissolved partnership retain the authority to do those things necessary to close down the existing partnership business. Under UPA Section 34, each partner is liable for his or her share of any liability created by partners in the course of closing down partnership business, just as if the partnership had not been dissolved.

3. Finally, there is actual termination of the business. Once the partnership has ended, no partnership business of any kind is legally authorized. If, after your partnership is dissolved, you have any doubts at all about the honesty of any of your partners, play it safe and notify all possible creditors. Just because you know that your partnership has been dissolved and your business wound up doesn't mean your creditors know it. If a creditor, acting in good faith and without knowledge of the dissolution of a partnership, extends credit to a partner, for matters that the partner represents as being partnership business, all the partners may be liable for that bill. Likewise, if a creditor extends credit to what he or she believes is the partnership, even after termination, you can be stuck for that

bill. UPA Section 35 effectively requires that to relieve partners of this liability, the partners must actually deliver notice of dissolution to all individuals or businesses who have previously extended credit to the partnership. A simple written letter, as given in the following example, is sufficient notice:

To Whom It May Concern, and All Creditors of the Partnership:

This is to inform you that the partnership was dissolved by a decision of the partners on _____ and no new partnership business is authorized after that date.

Sincerely,

_____

Termination Agreements

Commonly, when partnerships end—especially when the partners remain on reasonably good terms and have a good partnership agreement—things go easily as to major matters, such as the division of partnership assets. But as we've said, even in the best terminations, there are bound to be some things that you didn't foresee when you drafted your partnership agreement. To handle loose ends, prepare a separate termination agreement covering all matters in the breakup of the partnership. Be precise here. This is your final partnership document, and it's safer to pin everything down. (You'll find a sample termination agreement at the end of this chapter.)

If the partnership is broke and can't pay its bills, and at least one, but not all, of the partners is insolvent, the solvent partners must contribute additional amounts to cover all liabilities. If more than one partner is solvent, the solvent ones must contribute in the proportion that those partners shared in the partnership profits.

Sample Partnership Termination Agreement

_____(AT)_____ and _____(KC)_____ agree as follows:

I. RECITALS

1. PARTNERSHIP. AT and KC have been and are now partners doing business under the name of AT & KC ASSOCIATES, with its principal place of business in Oakland, California.

2. PARTNERSHIP AGREEMENT. The partners entered into said partnership and have continued in partnership under the provisions of an agreement in writing, dated _____, 20___.

3. DESIRE TO DISSOLVE. The partners now desire to adopt a plan for a sale of part of the partnership and of dissolution for their partnership and liquidation of its affairs, in two steps.

4. VALUATION. The partners agree that each partnership asset disclosed in the partnership balance sheet has a present fair market value equal to its book value to the partnership and that consideration in excess of book value reflected in this Agreement is attributable to goodwill not shown on the balance sheet.

II. DISSOLUTION

1. PURCHASE BY AT. AT hereby purchases forty-nine percent (49%) of the partnership interest of KC, and KC hereby sells and irrevocably assigns to AT the said forty-nine percent interest in consideration of: (A) AT's $5,500 negotiable promissory note in the form of Exhibit A hereto and (B) AT's agreement to hold KC free and harmless from all partnership debts and liabilities.

Sample Partnership Termination Agreement (continued)

2. GUARANTEED PAYMENTS. KC has received since January 1, 20____, and shall continue to receive through calendar year 20____, guaranteed payments from the partnership, by way of remuneration for services rendered, at the rate of $1,000 per month. Except for such guaranteed payments, KC shall receive no another amounts from the partnership.

3. AMENDMENT OF PARTNERSHIP AGREEMENT. The Agreement of Partnership is hereby amended to provide that from and after _____, 20____, AT alone shall exercise management and control over partnership decisions, and that from and after that date, the profits and losses of the partnership with corresponding items of taxable income or deductible loss will be shared ninety-nine percent (99%) for AT and one percent (1%) for KC.

4. COMPETITION PERMITTED. From and after _____, 20____, each partner shall be free to conduct consulting activities apart from the partnership, even to the extent of competing with the partnership.

5. INSURANCE. KC shall continue to receive health and automobile liability insurance coverage under the partnership's policies through December 31, 20____.

   Upon execution of this Agreement, KC shall be entitled to assume the life insurance policy on her life presently carried by the partnership.

6. LEASE. AT and KC both shall continue to be named a lessee under the existing lease for the partnership's present principal office. However, AT shall pay all rent accruing from and after _____, 20____.

7. ACCESS. KC shall, for the present term of the existing lease on the partnership's principal place of business, have full access to and use of an office in the partnership premises and access to its files.

Sample Partnership Termination Agreement (continued)

8. NAME. AT shall not use the partnership's name or any name confusingly similar thereto in any new business conducted by him following liquidation of the partnership.

   a. During the period from _____,20____, through _____,20____, either partner shall be entitled to refer to the partnership name solely for purposes of indicating transition from the partnership to his or her new business.

   b. After _____,20___, either partner's use of the partnership name shall be only to the extent necessary to identify prior projects that either has completed.

9. TERMINATION AND LIQUIDATION. On December 31, 20____, the partnership shall purchase KC's remaining one percent (1%) interest for a price of $_____ and the partnership shall be dissolved, liquidated, and terminated. Upon such termination and liquidation, AT shall own all of the assets of the partnership and shall satisfy all its debts and liabilities, subject to the restrictions on use of the partnership name as specified in Paragraph 8 of this Agreement. From December 31, 20____, on, except for the purposes of carrying out the liquidation of the partnership, neither of the partners shall do any further business nor incur any further obligations on behalf of the partnership.

III. LIQUIDATION

1. ACCOUNTING. As of December 31, 20____, the partners shall cause an accounting to be made by the then partnership accountants of all of the assets of the partnership and of the respective equities of the creditors and the partners in the assets as of the effective date of the dissolution.

Sample Partnership Termination Agreement (continued)

2. DISCLOSURE. Except as appears by the books of the partnership, each of the partners represents that he or she has not heretofore contracted any liability that can or may charge the partnership or the other partner, nor has he or she received or discharged any of the credits, monies, or effects of the partnership.

3. SETTLING ACCOUNTS. Upon completion of the accounting, the partners shall pay all of the liabilities of the partnership including those owing to the partners other than for capital in accordance with *[the applicable state law]*. Payment of liabilities owing to the partners shall include payment of profits for the current accounting period computed on the basis of actual cash receipts to completion of the accounting. All amounts received after completion of the accounting shall be the sole property of AT.

IV. EXECUTION AND ENFORCEMENT

1. SURVIVAL OF REPRESENTATIONS. The representations and agreements set forth herein shall be continuous and shall survive the taking of any accounting.

2. SUCCESSORS AND ASSIGNS. This Agreement shall inure to the benefit of and bind the successors, assigns, heirs, executors, and administrators of the partners.

Executed on _____, 20___, at Oakland, California.

_____

AT

_____

KC

Dissolution by Court Action

Under UPA Section 32, the courts have the power to order a dissolution leading to termination of a partnership for any of the reasons listed below, no matter what the partnership agreement provides:

- A partner has been declared mentally incompetent by judicial proceedings.
- A partner is incapable of performing his or her part of the partnership agreement.
- A partner has been guilty of conduct that prejudicially affects the carrying on of the business.
- A partner willfully or persistently commits a breach of the partnership agreement (or is generally a bad egg).
- The business can only be carried on at a continuing loss.
- Any other equitable reasons.

(Note that if you have an expulsion clause, you shouldn't have to worry about a court kicking out a bad partner; you can do it yourselves.)

Here are examples of some of the types of misconduct that the courts consider justifiable grounds to dissolve a partnership:

- failure to contribute initial capital funds urgently required by the business
- failure to account for proceeds of sales
- appropriation of partnership property to pay personal debts, or
- constant quarrels, irreconcilable differences, intoxication, or gambling.

A lawsuit over a partner's asserted misconduct will be disastrous (really—take our word for it). First of all, these aren't easy matters for the remaining partners to prove. The courts usually require a strong case for dissolving a partnership on grounds of the misconduct of a partner. They greatly dislike dealing with what they feel are trifling causes or temporary grievances. In any case, as we've urged before, lawsuits are generally horrendous. This situation should be unnecessary if you've provided for the expulsion of a partner. ●

Partnership Disputes:
Mediation and Arbitration

I f there's a serious disagreement between partners that can't be resolved by personal discussions and negotiations, you need a method in your partnership agreement for resolving the conflict. That's the purpose of Clause 11. The basic dispute resolution methods are mediation, arbitration, some combination of the two, or—as a last resort—litigation.

Mediation

Mediation is a process where an outside person—the mediator—attempts to assist two (or more) partners to solve their dispute themselves, by reaching a mutually satisfactory resolution. Unlike an arbitrator, a mediator has no power to impose a decision. Many people feel that mediation is the best way to resolve disputes because it's nonadversarial and encourages participants to arrive at their own compromise solution. Mediation's strength is that no partner feels that he or she wasn't treated fairly because the partners discuss, negotiate, and reach an agreement voluntarily. Mediation can be especially valuable where the people involved in a dispute will necessarily have some form of continuing relationship, as is often the case for partners or even ex-partners. This will clearly be the case if ex-partners are also relatives or members of a fairly small geographical or professional community.

The mediator's job is to assist the parties in communicating with each other, seeing the other's side, and, hopefully, helping them to reach a compromise. By its very nature, mediation is an informal process, without formal rules of evidence and other court-like protocols. Normally, if one person thinks something should be discussed, it is. Though mediation is informal, that does not mean it is totally unstructured. Normally, the process follows several stages: The mediator's opening statement explaining the process; the disputants' opening statements; joint discussion; private meetings with the mediator (often called "caucuses"); joint negotiation; and finally, closure.

Should Your Partnership Agreement Require Counseling?

You can also include in your agreement a clause requiring counseling, good-faith discussions, or other methods aimed at resolving disputes. Personally, we're sympathetic to the motives partners have in including these provisions in their agreements and are optimistic that, in some situations, they may serve to remind the partners of their commitments to one another if a dispute arises. However, we must also say that we're skeptical about the value of requiring these methods in addition to or (worse) as a substitute for a good, tight mediation/arbitration clause. Why? If all partners want to use other means to resolve a conflict, they'll go ahead and do it. But if feelings get truly ruffled and one or more partners refuses to be reasonable, you'll need more than a vague statement about good-faith discussion to achieve a settlement.

Once the parties arrive at their own solution through mediation, the agreement is normally put in writing, and it becomes a legally binding contract.

The most important decision you'll make when including a mediation clause in your partnership agreement is deciding on the mediator. You can postpone this decision until a dispute actually occurs, but we feel it's usually better to decide who you'll have as a mediator at the beginning. You can always change your mediator later on, if all agree to. But if you do fall into a dispute you can't resolve yourselves, you don't want to fight over who your mediator shall be.

If there's someone you know and trust who's served others as a mediator, that person is likely to be a wise choice for you. Some lawyers have established legal practices devoted solely to mediating disputes and do an excellent job. Or, in some situations, you may want to designate a mediator with some technical expertise. For example, if your business involves complicated machinery, you may prefer a mediator who understands how these machines work.

If there is a dispute, the partners decide, along with the mediator, what issues need to be resolved. Together you and your partners also decide the rules of the proceeding. Generally, we don't believe it's sensible to set out details of a mediation proceeding in your partnership agreement. You ultimately will have to cooperate to resolve the dispute, and cooperating over procedural details can be a good place to start. But if you are comforted by pinning down some details now, go ahead and include them in your mediation clause.

If you ever decide to mediate a dispute, here are some basic things you'll then need to resolve about the proceeding:

- When and where will the proceeding take place?
- Will you limit or require the number of sessions?
- Will you be allowed to submit a written statement?
- Will attorneys or other representatives be allowed, or will each partner represent himself or herself?
- Is cross-examination allowed?

Following is a clause you can use or adapt if you decide you want mediation of disputes you can't resolve privately:

Mediation

1. The partners agree that, except as otherwise provided in this Agreement, any dispute arising out of this Agreement or the partnership business shall first be resolved by mediation, if possible. The partners are aware that mediation is a voluntary process, and pledge to cooperate fully and fairly with the mediator in any attempt to reach a mutually satisfactory compromise to a dispute.

2. The mediator shall be _____.

3. If any partner to a dispute feels it cannot be resolved by the partners themselves after mediation has been effected, he or she shall so notify the other partners, and the mediator, in writing.

[If you prefer, you can vary this to require there be a set number of mediation sessions, so the disgruntled partner must say to all, face-to-face, that he or she won't agree to a mediation solution.]

4. Mediation shall commence within _____ days of this notice of request for mediation.

[Here, in #4, you can add any other details of the mediation process you've decided to include.

_____

_____

_____

_____

_____

_____

_____*.]*

5. Any decision reached by mediation shall be reduced to writing, signed by all partners, and be binding on them.

6. The costs of mediation shall be shared equally by all partners to the dispute.

Arbitration

We believe that it's essential to include an arbitration clause in all partnership agreements. The basics of the arbitration process should be set out in your arbitration clause. If arbitration is ever called for, the arbitrator determines any other specifics of the process that all partners can't voluntarily agree on.

In an arbitration proceeding, both sides present their version of the dispute to the arbitrator. After the presentation, the arbitrator later makes a decision, normally in writing, which ends the dispute. All partners are bound by the arbitrator's decision, with very rare exceptions. If the losing partners decide to sue in court to overturn the arbitrator's decision (which seldom happens), the court will usually enforce the artbitrator's decision.

Below are two arbitration clauses. In the first, there's a single arbitrator. In the second, there are three arbitrators: Each side selects one arbitrator and then those two select a third. All three hear the matter and decide it by majority vote.

Our preference is to use the first clause and one arbitrator. It's much simpler and cheaper. On the other hand, with three arbitrators, each side has chosen one who, presumably, is "on his side."

If you decide to select the clause using three arbitrators, you can't name the three arbitrators now, because, obviously, you can't predict which partners will be on what side. However, you do need to decide now what would happen if the two arbitrators cannot agree on a third. So think of some method to handle that problem—like naming someone now all partners trust to make the decision.

If you select the clause using one arbitrator, you can either name that person now, or wait. We suggest it's preferable to name one now, for the persuasive reason that you should all be able to agree on whom to select. If the need for arbitration ever actually arises, that agreement is likely to be more difficult, or even impossible, to obtain.

Whom do you select as your arbitrator? There's no one way to go about this that's inherently better than all others. You can name an arbitrator who's a trusted friend. Selecting a friend can result in some problems, however, if the friend later rules against you. Or, you may know someone who, although not a close friend, seems fair and capable of judiciously deciding matters (and of course, is willing to take on the job). Another possibility is someone who has served as an arbitrator before. Many lawyers frequently serve as arbitrators, as do other professional dispute resolvers. Also, in many areas of the country, retired judges serve as arbitrators. One caveat about professional arbitrators: Some, such as those from the American Arbitration Association, are quite expensive. Check fees before you agree on any expert. If you require specific rules for the arbitration proceeding, be sure the arbitrator or arbitration organization you choose will accept your rules. For example, the American Arbitration Association requires the use of their own detailed rules.

If you choose a combined mediation-arbitration clause, as we urge, you need to decide if you want to name the same person as both your arbitrator and your mediator. Some people decide that giving the mediator the power to impose a decision if the partners can't agree is a bad idea. Others decide that this risk is more than offset by the fact that there can only be one proceeding, not two.

Here are two arbitration clauses. The first uses one arbitrator. The second uses three. (If there are more than two sides to the conflict, the appointment of arbitrators becomes difficult. If you can't later get at least two of the sides to agree on one arbitrator, you'll probably wind up in court.) We believe it's preferable not to be more specific about the arbitration process in this clause. Leave that up to the arbitrator and yourselves, if the need ever arises. But if you want more specifics now, you can modify either clause, and specify more details of the arbitration process, including:

- Can the arbitrator order you to produce evidence? (Normally an arbitrator has this power.)
- Does the arbitrator have to explain the decision (that is, how and why the arbitrator reached it)?
- Is there a time limit within which the arbitrator must render a decision?
- Will you be allowed to submit a written statement?
- Is cross-examination allowed?
- Will lawyers be allowed?

Arbitration With One Arbitrator

1. The partners agree that, except as otherwise provided in this Agreement, any dispute arising out of this Agreement, or the partnership business, shall be arbitrated under the terms of this clause. The arbitration shall be carried out by a single arbitrator [who shall be _____ name _____] [or, if you don't want to name the arbitrator now, delete the phrase "who shall be ," and type in: "who shall be agreed upon by the parties to the dispute. If the parties cannot agree on the arbitrator, the arbitrator shall be selected by _____." Include the method you decide on, such as naming a person all agree now is fair to select the arbitrator.]

Any arbitration shall be held as follows:

2. The partner(s) initiating the arbitration procedure shall inform the other partner(s) in writing of the nature of the dispute at the same time that he or she notifies the arbitrator.

3. Within _____ days from receipt of this notice, the other partners shall reply in writing, stating their view of the nature of the dispute.

4. The arbitrator shall hold a hearing on the dispute within seven (7) days after the reply of the other partner(s). Each partner shall be entitled to present whatever oral or written statements he or she wishes and may present witnesses. No partner may be represented by a lawyer or any third party.

5. The arbitrator shall make his or her decision in writing.

6. If the partner(s) to whom the demand for arbitration is directed fails to respond within the proper time limit, the partner(s) initiating the arbitration must give the other an additional five (5) days' written notice of "intention to proceed to arbitration." If there is still no response, the partner(s) initiating the arbitration may proceed with the arbitration before the arbitrator, and his or her award shall be binding.

7. The cost of arbitration shall be borne by the partners as the arbitrator shall direct.

8. The arbitration award shall be conclusive and binding on the partners and shall be set forth in such a way that a formal judgment can be entered in the court having jurisdiction over the dispute if any partner so desires.

Now here's the clause where each side names his or her own arbitrator, and those two name a third.

Arbitration With Three Arbitrators

The partners agree that, except as otherwise provided in this Agreement, any dispute arising out of this Agreement or the partnership business shall be arbitrated under the terms of this clause. The arbitration shall be carried out by three arbitrators. Each partner or side to the dispute shall appoint one arbitrator. The two designated arbitrators shall appoint the third arbitrator.

The arbitration shall be carried out as follows:

1. The partner(s) initiating the arbitration procedure shall inform the other partner(s) in writing of the nature of the dispute at the same time that they designate one arbitrator.

2. Within ____ days from receipt of this notice, the other partners shall reply in writing, naming the second arbitrator and stating their view of the nature of the dispute.

3. The two designated arbitrators shall name a third arbitrator within ten (10) days from the date the second arbitrator is named. If they cannot agree *[insert whatever you've decided upon to resolve this dilemma]*.

4. An arbitration meeting shall be held within ____ days after the third arbitrator is named.

5. Each partner shall be entitled to present whatever oral or written statements he or she wishes and may present witnesses. No partner may be represented by a lawyer or any third party.

6. The arbitrators shall make their decision in writing.

7. If the partner(s) to whom the demand for arbitration is directed fails to respond within the proper time limit, the partner(s) initiating the arbitration must give the other an additional five (5) days' written notice of "intention to proceed to arbitration." If there is still no response, the partner(s) initiating the arbitration may proceed with the arbitration before the arbitrators, and their award shall be binding.

8. The cost of arbitration shall be borne by the partners as the arbitrators shall direct.

9. The arbitration award shall be conclusive and binding on the partners and shall be set forth in such a way that a formal judgment can be entered in the court having jurisdiction over the dispute if any partner so desires.

Combining Mediation With Arbitration

We believe it's usually desirable to have both a mediation and an arbitration clause in your agreement. That way, all partners know that they'll try mediation first. Only if that doesn't work out can an outside arbitrator impose a decision.

Some experienced lawyers feel it is unnecessary to bother with a compulsory mediation clause. They prefer to omit such a clause from the agreement, thus making mediation optional. The reason is as follows: If all partners want to mediate, they can, but if one of the partners isn't interested in mediating, why waste the time seeking a cooperative solution? Also, they believe that if mediation fails, things can be worse because tempers can become inflamed during mediation. We believe mediation can often work, and we think there is a greater possibility that it will if partners agree in advance to give it an honest chance.

If you only want one dispute resolution method in your agreement, select arbitration, because it must lead to a binding decision.

As we've mentioned, if you do follow our advice and choose both mediation and arbitration, you have to decide whether the mediator and arbitrator should be the same person. The obvious advantage to having the same person for both is that you don't run the risk of having to present the case twice—first to the mediator, then, if mediation fails, to the arbitrator. The other side of this coin is that a person who has ultimate power to make a decision as an arbitrator may be less effective as a mediator. Indeed, whether mediators should have the ultimate power to decide a dispute if the parties can't is an issue that divides many mediation professionals. Some feel that giving the mediator that much power ultimately destroys the voluntariness of the whole process. Others feel that a good dispute resolver can readily switch hats from mediator to arbitrator, and this is far preferable for all involved than risking a second go-round.

Here's a clause to bridge your mediation clause to your arbitration clause:

Combining Mediation With Arbitration

> If the partners cannot resolve the dispute by mediation, the dispute shall be arbitrated as provided in the arbitration clause of this Agreement.

The above clause doesn't set any express time limit on the mediation process. One side could simply quit and end the process. To eliminate the possibility of stalling, bad-faith mediation to drag out the time, you can add the following clause:

Time for Mediation

> If the partners have not resolved their dispute within [*whatever time you choose*] of the commencement of mediation, the partners shall have failed to have resolved their dispute by mediation under this Agreement, and the dispute shall be arbitrated.

Drafting Your Own Partnership Agreement

t's time to prepare your own partnership agreement. This chapter takes you step-by-step through each basic topic we believe you should cover in your agreement. You can download the Partnership Agreement from the Nolo website. (See Appendix B for instructions on how to do this.) A copy of the agreement is also included in Appendix C. If you have any doubts whether you want to include a specific clause in your agreement, turn back to the discussion of that clause in the appropriate chapter of the book.

How to Prepare Your Agreement

Follow the steps below to create your partnership agreement. When selecting which clauses to include in your agreement, follow these rules:

- Review Chapters 3 through 6, where each clause is explained in detail and information on how to complete them is provided.
- Work through all the sample clauses, checking the clauses you want to include and filling them in as appropriate.

Step 1: Select the Clauses You Want for Your Agreement

Almost all the clauses follow the order of the earlier chapters; however there are some exceptions we want to mention:

- In the Partnership Agreement, the clauses concerning the expulsion of a partner are included with those that deal with the continuity of partnership business should a partner leave or die. This is a slightly different approach than the one we took in Chapter 5, where we have a separate heading for expulsion clauses. We do not provide a separate heading for expulsion clauses here, since it's been our experience that few partners actually choose to include such a clause in their agreement.
- In the Partnership Agreement, Clause 12, General Provisions, includes some standard legal provisions that lawyers call boilerplate. These clauses are aptly called boilerplate because they

are routinely attached to most partnership agreements. These boilerplate clauses were not presented in the earlier text because they cover obvious matters you normally don't need to discuss.

For example, one of our boilerplate clauses states that your written agreement contains the entire understanding of the partners regarding their rights and duties in the partnership, and no alleged oral modification is valid. Perhaps this seems obvious, but if one partner subsequently tries to claim that an oral agreement between you has altered the written terms of this agreement, it will prove handy to have this boilerplate clause in your agreement.

Step 2: Finish the Clauses You've Selected

Now comes the vital task of completing all clauses you've selected. We want to remind you once again that this may involve more than simply filling in the blank lines of our sample clauses. Many partnership agreements require some modification and adaptation of our sample clauses to fit partners' specific situations.

EXAMPLE: In the sample agreement at the end of this chapter, Clause 4, CONTRIBUTIONS, contains some subclauses which adapt the clauses in the Partnership Agreement to their individual needs. Subclause 4.B, CASH CREDIT, adapts cash contribution provisions to an uncommon situation where one partner gets contribution credit for below-market rent of a building. And Subclause 4.C, CONTRIBUTION OUT OF PROFIT, adapts our subclause covering this issue to an individual situation. Our subclause provides that a partner shall not make any cash contribution, but shall make his or her entire contribution out of future profits. However, in the sample agreement, one partner is making some cash contributions at the beginning, so only part, but not all, of her total contribution will be paid out of future profits. Accordingly, these partners had to adapt our Partnership Agreement clauses to reflect what they were actually doing.

Hopefully, you made notes for the clauses you want, and kept track of any modifications or changes you need, when you read Chapters 3 through 6. You can use that information now as you complete your partnership agreement. Fill in all blank lines from the sample clauses that you use. And of course, you can always turn back to the text where a particular clause was first discussed if you have questions.

Here's an example of how you actually complete a clause. This is the initial clause in your agreement. You simply fill in the date you plan to sign your final, typed agreement, along with the names of the partners, as shown below.

> ☐ This Partnership Agreement is entered into and effective as of June 19, 20 xx
>
> by the partners _____ Eli Manstein _____ , _____ Alon Talmi _____ ,
>
> _____ Kathleen O'Brien. _____ .

TIP

Completing the general provisions. In the boilerplate clauses under 12, GENERAL PROVISIONS, you'll complete one clause you haven't seen before, where you list the name of the state whose laws will govern your partnership. This is usually the state where you live and will do business. If you plan to operate in more than one state, or the partners live in more than one state, you should normally select the state where you have your principal place of business.

Step 3: Complete Any New Clauses You've Prepared

If you've decided to create a new clause, different from any presented in this book, you will need to figure out the precise wording. If you have trouble doing this, or have any doubt as to a provision's legal effect, see a lawyer.

Drafting Two-Person Partnership Agreements

In preparing the partnership clauses set out in this chapter, we assumed there will be three or more partners. This means that if you're preparing an agreement for a two-person partnership, you have to make some minor changes to some of our clauses. For example, some buyout clauses refer to a "partnership," or "partners," that remains after one partner leaves. But if there were only two partners originally, and one departs, there's only one person left, so there can't be "remaining partners," or a "partnership." This means that when drafting an agreement for a two-person partnership, you will need to change these clauses to refer to the "remaining owner," as shown below.

☐ If any partner leaves the partnership, for whatever reason, whether he or she quits, withdraws, retires, or dies, his or her estate shall be obligated to sell his or her interest in the partnership to the <u>remaining owner</u>, who may buy that interest under the terms and conditions set forth in this Agreement.

If you are in a two-person partnership, read through each clause of your agreement with care to check that it is phrased correctly for you.

Step 4: Delete All Unnecessary Information

You will need to delete all extraneous material from the agreement you prepare.

Material that should be deleted includes:

- all clauses that you decide not to use
- any headings or subheadings you decide not to use
- all those little margin boxes, along with your check marks
- in clauses you complete, the blank lines (those you filled in or left blank), and
- any bracketed instructional material.

CAUTION

Do not delete the number and general caption for a basic clause.
For example, you should leave in headings such as:

"1. NAMES"

"2. TERMS"

"3. PURPOSE"

"4. CONTRIBUTIONS"

The reason you leave these in is because they identify the basic units of your agreement. You use them as the base for outlining your agreement as explained in Step 5, below.

Step 5: Outline Your Agreement

At the beginning of the document it says "Partnership Agreement," and then you list the names of the partners and the date of the agreement. This first clause is not given an identifying number, but after that, we have divided your agreement into basic units, each with a number and identifying caption:

"1. NAMES"

"2. TERM OF THE PARTNERSHIP"

"3. PURPOSE"

"4. CONTRIBUTIONS"

"5. PROFITS AND LOSSES"

"6. MANAGEMENT POWERS AND DUTIES" and so on.

Some of these basic units include subclauses. You will need to identify those subclauses with letters or numbers so that your agreement is structured coherently.

Following this approach, your contributions clause would look like this:

4. CONTRIBUTIONS

a. [Specific Cash Clause]

b. [Specific Property Clause]

There is no legal requirement that you have headings for your subclauses, but we've provided them, should you prefer this extra element of structure. If you do, your contributions clause could be structured as:

4. CONTRIBUTIONS

a. Cash
[Specific Cash Clause]

b. Property
[Specific Property Clause]

You may well have sub-subclauses. For example, you may have in your agreement:

4. CONTRIBUTIONS

a. Cash

(i) *cash contribution*
[specific cash contributions clause]

(ii) *initial work contribution*
[specific initial work contribution clause]

(iii) *extra cash loaned by a partner*
[specific cash loan clause]

You have considerable discretion as to how you outline and structure the subclauses (and sub-subclauses, and so on) of your agreement. As long as you come up with an order that is clear and works for all of you, you're fine.

Step 6: Prepare a Draft of Your Agreement

Once you've prepared a draft of your agreement, have it reviewed by all the partners. Make sure that all of your clauses fit together to make an orderly whole. You want to have an agreement that you all understand and that reads coherently.

Step 7: Prepare Your Final Agreement

Prepare your final agreement and have each partner sign and date the agreement at the end. The sample partnership agreement included at the end of this chapter is a good example of what a final partnership agreement looks like.

A partnership agreement doesn't have to be notarized unless it entails the ownership of real property and you want to record it at your local land title recording office. Each partner should be given a copy of the signed agreement. Keep the original in a safe place.

Sample Partnership Agreement

This Partnership Agreement is entered into and effective as of June 6, 20xx, by Laurie Mendez and Peter ("Pete") Johnston, the partners.

1. NAME

    The name of the partnership shall be: Mendez and Johnston.

    The name of the partnership business shall be: Crowbars.

2. TERM OF THE PARTNERSHIP

    The partnership shall last until it is dissolved by all the partners, or a partner leaves, for any reason, including death.

3. PURPOSES OF THE PARTNERSHIP

    The purpose of the partnership is to produce and sell Crowbars, high-quality climbers' food, and other high-quality food products.

    The specific purposes of the partnership are set out above. In addition, the goals and dreams of each partner are set out below. The partners understand that this statement is not legally binding, but include it in the Partnership Agreement as a record of their hopes and intentions. Both partners hope to create a prosperous business that sells a quality product, and which allows them to live the lives they want. Laurie wants to help provide for her family, including her children's college educations, and pay for travel. Pete wants to continue his mountain climbing, skiing, and travel.

4. CONTRIBUTIONS

    The initial capital of the partnership shall consist of the following:

    A. Cash Contributions

Name	Amount
Laurie Mendez	$13,000
Peter Johnston	$35,000

    Each partner's contribution shall be paid in full by July 10, 20xx.

Sample Partnership Agreement (continued)

B. Cash Credit

Laurie Mendez shall receive a credit of $5,000 toward her contribution because of the below-market rent provided by her uncle for the first year of the lease of the premises at 56 Holloway Street and $2,000 credit for use of her recipes.

C. Contribution Out of Profit

Laurie shall subsequently contribute to the partnership capital twenty-five percent (25%) of her share of the partnership profits for each fiscal year, beginning on the effective date of this agreement, until her total contribution, including cash and cash credit, equals Peter's.

D. Ownership of Partnership Business

Each partner's ownership share of the business shall be:

Name	Share
Laurie Mendez	50%
Peter Johnston	50%

5. PROFITS AND LOSSES

The partners will share all profits equally, and they will be distributed at least monthly. All losses of the partnership shall also be shared equally.

6. MANAGEMENT POWERS AND DUTIES

A. Skills Contributed

All partners shall be actively involved and materially participate in the management and operation of the partnership business.

Each partner named below shall participate in the business by working in the manner described: Laurie shall be in charge of the production of Crowbars. Peter shall be in charge of the marketing of Crowbars.

Sample Partnership Agreement (continued)

B. Partnership Decisions

All major decisions of the partnership business must be made by a unanimous decision of both partners. Minor business decisions may be made by an individual partner. Major decisions are defined as the expenditure of $1,000 or more.

C. Hours Worked

Except for vacations, holidays, and times of illness, each partner shall work at least thirty (30) hours per week on partnership business.

D. Leaves of Absence

Any partner can take a leave of absence from the partnership upon agreement by the other partner.

E. Accountings

1. Accounting on Request by a Partner:

Accountings of any aspect of partnership business shall be made upon written request by any partner.

2. Accountant to Determine Profits and Losses:

The partnership's net profit or net loss for each fiscal year shall be determined as soon as practicable after the close of that fiscal year. This should be done by a certified public accountant in accordance with the accounting principles employed in the preparation of the federal income tax return filed by the partnership for that year, but without a special provision for tax-exempt or partially tax-exempt income.

F. Outside Business Activities: Permitted, Except for Direct Competition

Any partner may be engaged in one or more other businesses as well as the business of the partnership, but only to the extent that this

Sample Partnership Agreement (continued)

activity does not directly and materially interfere with the business of the partnership and does not conflict with the time commitments and other obligations of that partner to the partnership under this Agreement. Neither the partnership nor any other partner shall have any right to any income or profit derived by a partner from any business activity permitted under this section.

G. Ownership of Business Assets

1. Trade Secrets:

    All trade secrets used or developed by the partnership, including customer lists and sources of supplies, will be owned and controlled by the partnership.

2. Business Name:

    The partnership name of Crowbars shall be partnership property. In the event of the departure of a partner, and/or dissolution of the partnership, control and ownership of the partnership name shall be determined pursuant to this Agreement.

7. TRANSFER OF A PARTNER'S INTEREST

A. Sale to Partnership at Its Option

    If either partner leaves the partnership, for whatever reason, whether he or she quits, withdraws, is expelled, retires, or dies, he or she or his or her estate shall be obligated to sell his or her interest in the partnership to the remaining owner, who may buy that interest, under the terms and conditions set forth in this Agreement.

B. The Partnership's Right to First Refusal Upon Offer From Outsiders

    If any partner receives a bona fide legitimate offer, whether or not solicited by him or her, from a person not a partner, to purchase all of his or her interest in the partnership, and if the partner receiving the

Sample Partnership Agreement (continued)

offer is willing to accept it, he or she shall give written notice of the amount and terms of the offer, the identity of the proposed buyer, and his or her willingness to accept the offer to the other partner. The other partner shall have the option, within thirty (30) days after the notice is given, to purchase that partner's interest on the same terms as those contained in the offer.

C. Refusal of the Remaining Partner to Buy

If the remaining partner does not purchase the departing partner's share of the business, under the terms provided in this Agreement, within thirty (30) days, the entire business of the partnership shall be put up for sale, and listed with the appropriate sales agencies, agents, or brokers.

D. Requiring Advance Notice of Withdrawal

Unless physically prevented from giving notice, a partner shall give sixty (60) days written advance notice of his or her intention to leave the partnership. If he or she fails to do so, the buyout price shall be reduced by twenty percent (20%).

8. BUYOUTS

A. The Asset Valuation Method

Except as otherwise provided in this Agreement, the value of the partnership shall be made by determining the net worth of the partnership as of the date a partner leaves, for any reason. Net worth is defined as the market value, as of that date, of the following assets:

1. All tangible property, real or personal, owned by the business;

2. All the liquid assets owned by the business, including cash on hand, bank deposits, and CDs or other monies;

Sample Partnership Agreement (continued)

3. All accounts receivable;

4. All earned but unbilled fees;

5. All money presently earned for work in progress;

6. Less the total amount of all debts owed by the business.

B. Revision of Valuation Method

The partners understand and agree that the preceding business valuation clause may not fully and adequately reflect the worth of the business after it has been successfully established, if the business has earned goodwill. Therefore, the partners agree that two (2) years after the commencement of the business they will amend this business valuation clause to include a method that will reflect any goodwill earned by the business.

C. Variation of the Buyout Price

The preceding method for calculating the value of the business shall be varied as stated below, for the reasons stated below:

If a partner leaves not for reasons of death, disability, or personal or family necessity, but to pursue other opportunities or plans, the buyout price shall be reduced thirty-five percent (35%).

D. Payment by Equal Monthly Payment

Whenever the partnership (or the remaining owner) is obligated or chooses to purchase a partner's interest, it shall pay for that interest by promissory note of the partnership. Any promissory note shall be dated as of the effective date of the purchase, shall mature in not more than five (5) years, shall be payable in equal installments that come due monthly, and shall bear interest at the rate of ten percent

Sample Partnership Agreement (continued)

(10%) per annum. The first payment shall be made sixty (60) days after the date of the promissory note.

9. CONTINUITY OF PARTNERSHIP BUSINESS

A. Control of Partnership Name

The partnership business name of Crowbars is owned by the partnership. Should any partner leave the business and desire to use the name Crowbars, and the remaining partner desires to continue the business and use the name Crowbars, ownership and control of the partnership business name shall be decided by mediation/arbitration.

10. MEDIATION AND ARBITRATION

A. Mediation

1. The partners agree that, except as otherwise provided in this Agreement, any dispute arising out of this Agreement or the partnership business shall first be resolved by mediation, if possible. The partners are aware that mediation is a voluntary process, and pledge to cooperate fully and fairly with the mediator in any attempt to reach a mutually satisfactory compromise to a dispute.

2. The mediator shall be as agreed on by the partners. If they cannot agree, the mediator shall be chosen by Catherine Howard, friend of both partners.

3. If any partner to a dispute feels it cannot be resolved by the partners themselves, he or she shall so notify the other partner, and the mediator, in writing.

4. Mediation shall commence within five (5) days of this notice of request for mediation.

Sample Partnership Agreement (continued)

5. Any decision reached by mediation shall be reduced to writing, signed by both partners, and be binding on them.

6. The costs of mediation shall be shared equally by all partners to the dispute.

B. Combining Mediation With Arbitration

If the partners cannot resolve the dispute by mediation, the dispute shall be arbitrated as provided in the arbitration clause of this Agreement.

C. Time for Mediation

If the partners have not resolved their dispute within thirty (30) days of the commencement of mediation, the partners shall have failed to have resolved their dispute by mediation under this Agreement, and the dispute shall be arbitrated.

D. Arbitration With One Arbitrator

1. The partners agree that, except as otherwise provided in this Agreement, any dispute arising out of this Agreement, or the partnership business, shall be arbitrated under the terms of this clause. The arbitration shall be carried out by a single arbitrator who shall be agreed upon by the partners to the dispute. If the partners cannot agree on the arbitrator, the arbitrator shall be selected by Catherine Howard.

Any arbitration shall be held as follows:

2. The partner initiating the arbitration procedure shall inform the other partner in writing of the nature of the dispute at the same time that he or she notifies the arbitrator.

3. Within seven (7) days from receipt of this notice, the other partner shall reply in writing, stating his or her views of the nature of the dispute.

Sample Partnership Agreement (continued)

4. The arbitrator shall hold a hearing on the dispute within seven (7) days after the reply of the other partner. Each partner shall be entitled to present whatever oral or written statements he or she wishes and may present witnesses. No person may be represented by a lawyer or any third party.

5. The arbitrator shall make his or her decision in writing.

6. If the partner to whom the demand for arbitration is directed fails to respond within the proper time limit, the partner initiating the arbitration must give the other an additional five (5) days' written notice of "intention to proceed to arbitration." If there is still no response, the partner initiating the arbitration may proceed with the arbitration before the arbitrator, and his or her award shall be binding.

7. The cost of arbitration shall be borne by the partners as the arbitrator shall direct.

8. The arbitration award shall be conclusive and binding on the partners and shall be set forth in such a way that a formal judgment can be entered in the court having jurisdiction over the dispute if either partner so desires.

11. AMENDMENTS

Amendment by Unanimous Agreement

This Agreement may be amended only by written consent of all partners.

12. GENERAL PROVISIONS

A. State Law

The partners have formed this general partnership under the laws of the State of Colorado, intending to be legally bound thereby.

Sample Partnership Agreement (continued)

B. Attached Papers Incorporated

Any attached sheet or document shall be regarded as fully contained in this Partnership Agreement.

C. Agreement Is All-Inclusive

This Agreement contains the entire understanding of the partners regarding their rights and duties in the partnership. Any alleged oral representations of modifications concerning this Agreement shall be of no force or effect unless contained in a subsequent written modification signed by all partners.

D. Binding on All Successors and Inheritors

This Agreement shall be binding on and for the benefit of the respective successors, inheritors, assigns, and personal representatives of the partners, except to the extent of any contrary provision in the Agreement.

E. Severability

If any term, provision, or condition of this Agreement is held by a court of competent jurisdiction to be invalid, void, or unenforceable, the rest of the Agreement shall remain in full force and effect and shall in no way be affected, impaired, or invalidated.

Signature: _*Laurie Mende*_____ Dated: _6/6/20xx_
Laurie Mendez

Signature: _*Peter Johnston*_____ Dated: _6/6/20xx_
Peter Johnston

Partnership and Taxes

Most start-up small business partnerships will not need to worry about complicated partnership tax law because it mostly involves complex enterprises with highly sophisticated tax matters. In putting this chapter together, we made judgment calls as to how deeply we should go into different areas of partnership taxation and reached two conclusions. First, partnership taxation is so complex that we will stick to the basics. Second, since the focus of this book is on starting a partnership, we concentrate on the likely tax problems faced by a new small business.

In the more complicated areas of partnership taxation, all we can safely do is alert you to warning signals and advise you to see a tax expert. Having access to a partnership tax expert is essential. This can be costly, but it is still cheaper and far less anxiety-ridden than risking a confrontation with the IRS.

Using Tax Experts

A tax expert in this context means someone experienced with and knowledgeable about IRS law and rules governing partnership taxation —and your state's partnership taxation rules, too. Realistically, this usually means a certified public accountant (CPA) with lots of small business experience, and more specifically, partnership tax experience.

Next question: Do you really need a tax expert? Most definitely. Unless your business is very simple, you should find a knowledgeable CPA and work out an arrangement to get the periodic help you'll need. In many—if not most—partnerships, it's beneficial to start a relationship with a tax expert as soon as you can. However, some truly uncomplicated partnerships might not need a tax expert's services immediately. For instance, a service business with very few inventory costs, in which all the partners contribute the same amount of start-up cash, might not need one immediately. But change a few facts—such as some partners contributing property that's appreciated in value since they bought it, or the necessity for a modest inventory—and you'll quickly find yourself needing expert advice.

Third question: Where do you find a high-quality, affordable partnership tax expert? If you happen to know one you trust, fine. If not, you will want to check with small business people in your area and see who they use. When it comes to expense, don't focus exclusively on how much the expert costs per hour. The key is to find an expert who will help you help yourself with routine matters, like establishing a good bookkeeping system. Once good systems are in place, you may only need to have them reviewed by your expert a few times a year.

> **ASK AN EXPERT**
>
> **Let Nolo take the guesswork out of finding a lawyer.** Nolo's Lawyer Directory (available at www.nolo.com) provides detailed profiles of attorney advertisers, including information about the lawyer's education, experience, practice area, and fees.

How Partnerships Are Taxed

The most basic tax rule on partnerships is that the partnership itself is not subject to taxation. A partnership is a pass-through entity, meaning the partnership's profits and losses simply flow through to the individual partners, who report the income (or loss) on their personal tax returns.

Partners' Distributive Share

Each partner is taxed on his or her distributive share of partnership income. A partner's distributive share is the portion of profits that partner is entitled to receive under the partnership agreement. This can be more than the profits or payments a partner actually receives if the partners decide to leave some of the profits in the business. Regardless of how much money they actually withdraw from the business, partners must pay taxes on their share of the partnership profits—total income minus expenses.

Business Deductions

Like any small business owner, partners are entitled to the many business deductions available under the Tax Code. Partners can deduct legitimate business expenses from their business income which can greatly reduce their taxable income. Deductible business expenses include items like start-up costs, operating expenses, and travel costs.

In addition to these business deductions, the Tax Cuts and Jobs Act created an important new tax deduction for pass-through business owners—including partners in partnerships (IRC Section 199A). Partners who qualify for the deduction can deduct up to 20% of their net business income from their income taxes, reducing their effective income tax rate by 20%. This is a personal deduction that partners take on their tax returns whether or not they itemize. There are certain restrictions on the deduction, including for businesses that provide personal services, but you will want to understand how this deduction works and take advantage of it if you can.

RESOURCE

Want to know more about deductions? For more in-depth information on how to make the most of business deductions, including the new 20% pass-through deduction, see *Tax Savvy for Small Business*, by Frederick W. Daily (Nolo), and *Deduct It! Lower Your Small Business Taxes*, by Stephen Fishman (Nolo).

Tax Reporting

Although a partnership doesn't have to pay tax, it must still file tax forms. Specifically, it must file an informational tax return, IRS Form 1065, *U.S. Return of Partnership Income*, listing its income and expenses. Also, the partnership must distribute to each partner a copy of Form 1095, and another IRS form, called Schedule K-1, *Partner's Share of Income, Credits, Deductions, etc.* Form K-1 states the distributive share a partner received. You can download these forms—as well as IRS Publication 541, *Partnerships*, which provides information on partnership taxation—at the IRS website, www.irs.gov. Most states also require partnerships to file an informational return; to find out your state's rules, contact your state taxing authority.

Tax Consequences of Contributions to a Partnership

The tax area that is usually of most concern to new partners involves contributions partners make when the business is just getting started. There are no tax problems if all partners contribute only cash—it's pretty clear how much each one contributed. No taxable gain or loss occurs simply because money is transferred from a partner to the partnership. Similarly, there's no taxable gain or loss if a partner withdraws some or all of the money he or she contributed to the partnership. (Withdrawing contributed capital is not the same as a partner's distributive share of partnership profits, which is taxable income to the partner who receives it.) But if a partner contributes property, especially property that has increased (or decreased) in value since it was purchased, the tax consequences of these transactions can become complicated. Likewise, there are complexities if a partner receives a partnership interest in exchange for a pledge of future services.

Contribution of Property

If a partner contributes property whose current market value is the same as what the partner originally paid for it, there's no tax problem. As with cash, no taxable transaction occurs merely because property is transferred from an individual owner to the partnership. But the tax situation is more complex if the property has gone up or down in value since the partner bought it.

EXAMPLE: Harry contributes a building he owns to a new partnership in exchange for a one-half partnership ownership share valued at $60,000. Jennifer, the other partner, contributes $60,000 in cash. If Harry recently bought the building for $60,000, there won't be any tax consequences. But suppose Harry bought the building years ago for $200,000. (The tax basis of a building to the owner is normally his acquisition cost, plus the cost of capital improvements, less any depreciation taken. Here we're assuming, for the sake of simplicity, that the original cost alone remained Harry's basis.) Because the building's market value is now $620,000, his partnership share is based on this amount. Does this mean that Harry has now realized a gain, for tax purposes, of $420,000, as if he'd "sold" the building in exchange for his partnership share? The answer is no. The tax code provides that when a partner contributes property to a partnership that's worth more than he or she paid for it, no immediate gain or loss is recognized to the partner. (I.R.C. Section 721.)

This sounds fine so far, but as you might expect, tax situations don't always stay so simple. To continue the above example, there can still be eventual tax consequences because the building was transferred to the partnership. For instance, because no taxable gain or loss is recognized on the transfer from Harry to the partnership, the tax basis of the building to the partnership is the same as Harry's basis, that is, $200,000. Now, let's suppose that the partnership decides to sell the building for its market value of $620,000. For tax purposes, the partners have realized a taxable gain of $420,000. But for purposes of partnership bookkeeping, there's been no gain or loss because a $620,000 partnership asset has been traded for a like amount of cash.

This is where the problems begin. If the taxable gain (the $420,000 profit) is divided equally between the two partners, Jennifer will have to pay tax on a gain of $200,000 even though she hasn't received any income. So the tax code now provides that the partner who contributed the appreciated property is regarded as receiving all of that built-in profit from a subsequent sale. This issue can get very complex, especially if the partnership held the property for a time and there was further appreciation. It's yet another area where you need to see a tax expert.

Contribution of Mortgaged Property

There are other potentially complex tax problems involving contributed property. We don't go into these in depth because we think few people establishing new partnerships will face them. Here, we highlight just a few areas that may affect you.

Taxes can get complicated if a partner contributes real estate with an outstanding mortgage or any encumbered property, such as a car with a loan balance owed. If mortgaged or encumbered property is contributed to a partnership, the partnership's liabilities are increased by the amount of the debt. (Technically, the property can be transferred subject to the mortgage, or the partnership can formally assume the mortgage. In either case, the tax issue is the same.) If a partner is contributing mortgaged or encumbered property, see a partnership tax expert.

Alternatives to Contributing Property

For a variety of reasons, partners may want their partnership to acquire property from a partner by a method other than contribution. For example, a partner may be willing to allow the partnership to use valuable property that partner owns, such as a patent, but be unwilling to contribute that property outright to the partnership. Or, the partnership may want to use real estate a partner owns without having to acquire that property.

A partner can legally engage in all legitimate property transactions with the partnership, such as sale, lease, or loan. Business transactions such as these between a partner and the partnership can get complicated. For example, a partner can sell a partial interest to other partners, and then each partner can contribute his or her interest to the partnership. A partner can lease, rent, or lend property to the partnership, or combine these methods. When contemplating any of these types of transactions, see a partnership tax expert.

Real Estate Exchanges

Here's one more potential partnership trap for real estate owners. As most real estate investors know, the tax code permits tax-free exchanges of real estate. (See I.R.C. Section 1031.) You can sell one parcel, buy another for what you sold the first parcel for (or more), and not be subject to any tax. This allows you to roll over any profits from sale of the first property into the second.

However, IRS rules require that the same type of legal entity be both the seller of the first property and the buyer of the second. If a partnership sells the first property, but a partner individually buys the second, that doesn't qualify. Likewise, if a partner sells one property, but a partnership buys another, that doesn't qualify. So you have to think through how you are going to handle both transactions before engaging in a tax-free real estate exchange, and be sure the same type of legal entity engages in both deals.

Contribution of Services

Now let's look at the tax consequences if a person receives an interest in a partnership in return for the contribution of services. Under the tax laws, services aren't property. If the contributing partner receives a capital (ownership) interest in the partnership in exchange for (the promise of) services, that partner has received taxable income.

> **EXAMPLE:** Alicia, Rose, and Ruby form a partnership to operate a consulting business. Alicia and Ruby each contribute $90,000 for start-up capital and plan to work part time in the business. Rose has no cash to contribute, but she receives a one-third ownership of the partnership in exchange for promising to work full time for a year. As far as the tax laws are concerned, Rose has received present taxable income by this agreement. The cash contributions to the business total $180,000; Rose owns one-third of the business. According to tax law, Rose has received taxable income of $60,000.

Unfortunately, Rose hasn't really received any money. If the business was sold, and she got one-third of the cash for the sale, it would be easier for her to pay tax on her share. But here, the tax code essentially treats her partnership interest as payment for her work (income).

If you're considering giving a partner an ownership interest, or even the right to receive future profits in exchange for services, see a CPA. One possibility to evaluate is hiring the would-be partner as an employee and paying enough so he or she can save up and buy a partnership interest outright for cash.

In more involved service contribution situations, the tax rules can become extremely complicated. If your partnership profits will involve this kind of problem, it's essential that you see a tax expert. Here are some examples of complicated situations.

Appreciated Partnership Property. In exchange for services to be rendered, a partner receives an interest in partnership property that has appreciated in value since being acquired by the partnership.

Restrictions on Transfers of a Partnership Interest. Special tax rules govern partnership interests exchanged for promised services if there are certain restrictions on the service partner, such as an agreement to sell his or her interest to the other partners for less than market value if the partner ceases performing the services.

Management of the Partnership Business

As anyone in business soon learns, tax concerns are part of your life. Aside from ongoing tax matters, there are some initial operating tax issues you'll need to discuss and review with your tax expert. These include:

- what accounting method you'll use (accrual, cash, or other permitted methods)
- what depreciation method you'll use for partnership property, and
- what the partnership's tax year should be.

As your business grows, it can be particularly important to determine whether there are tax or financial reasons for varying the way partnership income is distributed to partners. Tax laws allow any partnership income, profit, loss, or deduction to be distributed between partners in a way that is different from their standard division if: (1) that's permitted in the partnership agreement, and (2) this particular distribution has "substantial economic effect." (See I.R.C. Section 704(b)(2).) It takes an expert to figure out whether varying your income or profit figures is going to be beneficial for all involved (or, at least, overall). We don't cover this type of sophisticated maneuvering in this book, nor do the partnership agreements we provide have clauses covering ways in which to vary the normal distribution of profits, income, and so on, for tax purposes. If this proves advantageous years down the road, you can always amend your partnership agreement to include exactly the magic words tax law then requires. It's fully legal and acceptable to the IRS to make such later amendments if you decide to.

Tax Returns

The partnership and the partners have tax paperwork obligations:
1. The partnership must file an informational partnership tax return (Form 1065).
2. The partnership must provide each partner with a copy of Form 1065 and Schedule K-1, which breaks down each partner's share of partnership profits and losses.
3. Partners must report their share of partnership income on their individual tax returns.

The Partnership Tax Return

A partnership itself isn't subject to income tax. Income and profits generated by a partnership business flow through the partnership and are taxed to the individual partners. Nevertheless, a partnership must file an "informational" federal tax return, called IRS Form 1065, *U.S. Return of Partnership Income.* This return lists the partnership income, expenses, and other required financial data, many of which must be separately identified. This way, you report all the basic economic facts about your partnership, in addition to the net income reported on each partner's individual return. The Internal Revenue Service publishes free aids to completing a partnership tax return, including Publication 541, *Partnerships*, and Publication 334, *Tax Guide for Small Business*.

The yearly federal partnership return must be filed by the 15th day of the fourth month following the close of the partnership tax year.

Most states also require an informational partnership return to be filed. Like the federal government, the states don't tax partnership income per se.

The Partner's Individual Tax Return

We don't have the space to thoroughly explain the intricacies that can be involved in reporting your share of partnership income on your individual tax return. However, there are a few points worth mentioning.

Self-Employment Taxes

The federal government, and most states, consider most partners of a partnership to be "self-employed." Self-employed people don't have an employer to withhold income taxes from each paycheck, so partners must file quarterly estimates of their taxable income on Form 1040-ES, along with the appropriate tax payments. Generally, you must make estimated tax payments if you owe at least $1,000 and any tax withheld will be less than 90% of the tax you'll owe or 100% of last year's tax bill. If you don't make these quarterly payments (in April, June, September, and January), you can be subject to fines and penalties. While it can be difficult to figure out ahead of time how much tax you'll owe, as a general rule, you can make payments equal to your tax liability for the previous year. You can also purchase tax preparation software, such as Intuit's *TurboTax* program, to help you estimate these amounts.

In addition, each partner must also make quarterly estimated payments of his or her own self-employment taxes, which includes Social Security and Medicare. Right now, these amount to 15.3% of the first $137,700 of income (2020). Fortunately, a portion of these self-employment taxes is deductible, so this relieves some of the tax bite. As with the estimated income tax payments discussed above, the main thing to keep in mind is that you'll have to pay these taxes whether the partnership actually distributes this money to you or not, so plan ahead.

Other Income Tax Considerations

On top of self-employment taxes, here are some more partnership tax rules that affect your personal income taxes:

- An individual partner's yearly tax return must report a partner's distributive share of the taxable income or loss of the partnership.
- A partner's distributive share of partnership profits is, in part, determined by the partnership agreement. If the agreement doesn't mention how particular income, gains, losses, depreciation, or credits are to be allocated, a partner's distributive share is determined by the IRS in accordance with the provision of the partnership agreement for division of general profits or losses.
- The IRS will disregard special provisions as to distributive shares of partnership profits if it determines that the provision lacks "substantial economic effect" (that is, it has been adopted for the sole purpose of dodging taxes by shifting tax liability to partners in a lower tax bracket). In that case, the IRS will reallocate distributive shares according to the partners' ownership interest in the partnership. If you are interested in making special allocations, consult a partnership tax expert.
- There are special income tax rules governing allocations of partnership interest to individual partners to or with whom one partner sells or exchanges his or her partnership interest, or if there's a shift of the percentage of ownership interest (or sharing of profits and losses) during the year (see I.R.C. Section 706(c)). If this happens to you, you'll certainly need tax assistance.
- Each partner also takes his or her share of any loss into account each year. It may become part of the partner's carryback or carryforward for tax purposes (see I.R.C. Section 172), used to offset positive income in other years.
- If a partner has a "subpartnership" contract, sharing partnership profits with someone who is not a member of the partnership, the partner is still required to report as income the entire amount of the profits he or she was entitled to receive from the

partnership. The partner can take a deduction for the share allocated to the subpartner.

- Tax law provides different tax treatment for earned, investment, and passive income. If you plan to actively participate in your business, there is no need to worry about this. If you have any doubts or questions concerning these types of income, see a tax expert. And, if you're looking for tax shelters, be wary. We certainly know people who invested in so-called tax shelters that eventually backfired and cost them a lot of money.

- As pass-through business entity owners, partners in a partnership may be able to deduct 20% of their business income with the 20% pass-through deduction established under the Tax Cuts and Jobs Act.

The Partnership as a Separate Tax Entity

For income tax purposes, a partnership is basically a conduit allowing income to pass through to the individual partners. However, as is so common in the tax field, there are some qualifications, exceptions, and but-ifs. To be more specific, for certain purposes, a partnership isn't treated as a conduit but is viewed as a distinct entity by the IRS. For example:

- For computation of partnership income—profits and losses—a partnership is regarded as a unified enterprise. In other words, whether a profit or loss has been made is determined by looking to the partnership as a whole, not to any individual partner.

- The partnership itself, not the partners, must make certain tax elections, such as the choice of accounting method.

- In the unusual instance in which a partner has a different tax year than the partnership, whether an item or distributive share of income or loss should be included in a partner's tax return will depend on the tax year of the partnership itself.

- The characterization of business income, whether earned or passive, is made at the partnership level, not at each partner's level.

Taxation and Sale of a Partnership Interest

The sale of a partnership interest has tax consequences. On the simplest level, a partner who sells a partnership interest will receive income from the sale and be subject to tax on that income. However, tax problems related to the disposition of a partnership interest can become much more complex. Because this is a book designed for those beginning a partnership, we don't go into these possible complexities in detail. You should know that if your business is successful and some time in the future a partner wants to sell, retires, or dies, you can avail yourself of any tax options permitted to you within that year of sale. In other words, you're not now locked into anything that could have adverse tax consequences later.

Termination of a Partnership on Transfer of a Partnership Interest

You do not want your partnership considered legally terminated unless in fact it truly is—that is, the business is over and all partners are out of it. (Special rules apply to two-person partnerships—see below.) If only one or some partners leave the partnership, tax reasons alone make it desirable to have the partnership continue. If the partnership is formally terminated, all partnership properties are considered distributed to the partners. Distributed means that the IRS regards the property received as income to the partners, so any gain received by the partners will be taxed. This can be very undesirable for property that has increased in value since acquisition by the partnership.

> EXAMPLE: A four-person partnership buys a piece of real estate for $160,000. Ten years later, the market value of the real estate is $480,000. The partnership has made a paper profit of $320,000, or $80,000 per partner. One partner leaves, selling his interest to a new person. The other partners remain, continuing the business. They do not want to sell the real estate, which they use in the business. Unfortunately, the partnership agreement provides that the partnership is terminated if any partner leaves. Because the old partnership has technically been terminated, the IRS considers all the profits on the

real estate as having been distributed to the partners. Each partner's profit is $80,000. If they don't want to sell the real estate, they must each come up with the cash from somewhere else to pay taxes due on their $80,000.

Because of this risk, we've provided you a clause (Clause 10), which we urge you to include in your agreement, stating that the partnership continues and is not dissolved or terminated if a partner, or partners, leaves the business. (See Chapter 5.)

Sale of 50% or More of a Partnership

The sale of an interest of 50% or more of partnership capital or the right to receive profits raises immediate tax problems. No matter what the partnership agreement says, tax law provides that such a sale results in the distribution of all partnership property to the partners. There's no easy way to escape this rule, though tax experts surely try.

This rule can create hardships for a two-person partnership. In a two-person, 50-50 partnership, sale of either partner's interest obviously terminates the partnership. But if one partner buys out the other, the rule that all partnership property is distributed can lead to very unfair results. It can be difficult enough for the buying partner to pay for the other's share without also having to pay tax on the buying partner's own share if that share will actually be left in the business. Happily, tax law recognizes this reality, so the tax rule is different if one partner buys out another. In that case, the partnership can, if the remaining partner so desires, be regarded as continuing. The Internal Revenue Code provides that when payments are made by a remaining partner to a retiring partner of a two-person 50-50 partnership, that partner will be regarded as remaining in the partnership until his or her entire interest is liquidated. (See I.R.C. Section 736.) This rule applies even if state law specifically provides that the partnership has been terminated on sale. Without this federal tax law, the partner continuing the business would have to pay income taxes on his or her own interest in the business when the other partner retired—an unfair burden to impose on one who wants to continue an existing business, not cash it out.

Sale or Buyout of a Partner's Interest

The details of an actual sale or purchase of a partner's interest should not be finalized without consulting a tax expert. There are a number of tax options you need to consider, most of which can be handled at the time—or near the time—of the transaction. For example, I.R.C. Section 754 permits the partnership to adjust the basis of certain partnership assets when a new partner buys into the partnership. The partnership must make the election to adjust the basis of these assets in the year when the sale occurs.

The partnership tax year for the selling partner (only) closes on the date of the sale. The selling partner's share in net partnership income or loss for that period must be reported on his or her tax return for that tax year. The IRS permits the use of "reasonable" estimates by the partners to determine that income. This reasonable estimate can be made by agreement of the partners in the year of the sale.

> **EXAMPLE:** John sells his one-third interest in the Alice-John-Joan partnership on March 1. The partnership is on a January 1 to December 31 fiscal year, and profits are determined quarterly. Under the IRS rules, John's tax year for his partnership interest closes on the date of sale—March 1. But what is his portion of partnership profits for the two months he was a partner that year? They haven't yet been calculated, so the partners can make a reasonable estimate of the profits to which John is entitled.

Retirement or Death of a Partner

Here are a few things you should know about tax consequences when a partner retires or dies:

- Payments made in exchange for a partner's partnership interest that are considered a distribution of partnership profits are not deductible to the partnership as a business expense. They are, of course, taxable income to the partner.

- The valuation placed on a retiring partner's interest in an arm's length, or bona fide, transaction will normally be accepted by the IRS.
- If a partnership business is to be terminated completely, with all assets sold and the enterprise liquidated, complex tax rules are involved, and (we'll say it one more time) you should see a partnership tax expert.

RESOURCE

For more on partnerships and taxes, see *Federal Taxation of Partnerships and Partners,* by Robert L. Whitmire, William F. Nelson, and William S. Mckee (Warren, Gorham & Lamont).

Also useful for business tax matters:

- *Partnership Taxation,* by Arthur B. Willis, John S. Pennell, and Phillip F. Postlewaite (McGraw-Hill)
- IRS Publication 334, *Tax Guide for Small Business,* and if you're just getting started, IRS Publication 583, *Starting a Business and Keeping Records,* and
- *U.S. Master Tax Guide* (CCH, Inc.). Updated annually, it features in-depth explanations of many tax complexities.

Citations to State Uniform Laws

Citations to State Uniform Laws	
The Uniform Partnership Act and the 1997 Uniform Partnership Act*	
State	**Statutory Citation**
*Alabama	Al. St. 1975, §§ 10-8A-101 to 10-8A-1109
*Alaska	A.S. §§ 32.05.010 to 32.05.430 and 32.06.201 to 32.06.997
*Arizona	A.R.S. §§ 29-1001 to 29-1111
*Arkansas	A.C.A. §§ 4-46-101 to 4-46-1207
*California	West's Ann. Cal. Corp. Code §§ 16100 to 16962
*Colorado	West's C.R.S.A. §§ 7-64-101 to 7-64-1206
Connecticut	N/A
*Delaware	6 Del. C. §§ 15-101 to 15-1210
*District of Columbia	D.C. Official Code, 2001 Ed. §§ 33-101.01 to 33-112.04
*Florida	West's F.S.A. §§ 620.81001 to 620.8908
Georgia	O.C.G.A. §§ 14-8-1 to 14-8-43
*Hawaii	H.R.S. §§ 425-101 to 425-145
*Idaho	I.C. §§ 53-3-101 to 53-3-1205
*Illinois	106 Ill. Comp. Stat. Ann. §§ 205/100 to 206/1207
Indiana	Ind. Code Ann. §§ 23-4-1-1 to 23-4-1-43
*Iowa	I.C.A. §§ 486A.101 to 486A.1302
*Kansas	K.S.A. §§ 56A-101 to 56A-1305
*Kentucky	K.R.S. §§ 362.1-101 to 362.1-1205
*Maine	31 M.R.S.A. §§ 1001 to 1105
*Maryland	Code, Corporations and Associations, §§ 9A-101 to 9A-1205
Massachusetts	M.G.L.A. Ch. 108A, §§ 1 to 44
Michigan	M.C.L.A. §§ 449.1 to 449.43

Citations to State Uniform Laws (continued)

The Uniform Partnership Act and the 1997 Uniform Partnership Act*

*Minnesota	M.S.A. §§ 323A.0101 to 323A.1203
*Mississippi	Code 1972, §§ 79-12-1 to 79-12-85
Missouri	V.A.M.S. §§ 358.010 to 358.430
*Montana	M.C.A. §§ 35-10-101 to 35-10-644
*Nebraska	R.R.S. 1943, §§ 67-301 to 67-343 and 67-401 to 67-467
*Nevada	N.R.S. §§ 87.010 to 87.430
New Hampshire	R.S.A. §§ 304-A:1 to 304-A:62
*New Jersey	N.J.S.A. §§ 42:1A-1 to 42:1A-56
*New Mexico	N.M.S.A. 1978, §§ 54-1-47, 54-1A-101 to 54-1A-1206
New York	McKinney's Partnership Law, §§ 1 to 75
North Carolina	G.S. §§ 59-31 to 59-73
*North Dakota	N.D.C.C. §§ 45-13-01 to 45-21-08
*Ohio	R.C. §§ 1776.01 to 1776.96
*Oklahoma	54 Okl. St. Ann. §§ 1-100 to 1-1207
*Oregon	O.R.S. §§ 67.005 to 67.810 and 68.010 to 68.650
Pennsylvania	15 PA Code, Title 15, Chapter 84
Rhode Island	Gen. Laws 1956, §§ 7-12-12 to 7-12-55
South Carolina	Code 1976, §§ 33-41-10 to 33-41-1090
*South Dakota	S.D.C.L. §§ 48-7A-101 to 48-7A-1208
*Tennessee	T.C.A. §§ 61-1-101 to 61-1-142
*Texas	Vernon's Ann. Texas Civ. St. art. 6132b, §§ 1.01-10.05
*Utah	U.C.A. §§ 48-16-101 to 48-16-1205
*Vermont	11 V.S.A. §§ 3201 to 3313
*Virginia	Code 1950, §§ 50-73.79 to 50-73.149
*Washington	West's R.C.W.A. 25.05.005 to 25.05.907
*West Virginia	Code, §§ 47B-1-1 to 47B-10-5
Wisconsin	W.S.A. §§ 178.01 to 178.39
*Wyoming	W.S. 1977, §§ 17-21-101 to 17-21-1002

*States that have adopted the 1997 UPA are indicated with an asterisk.

How to Use the Downloadable Forms on the Nolo Website

This book comes with downloadable files that you can access online at:

www.nolo.com/back-of-book/PART.html

To use the files, your computer must have specific software programs installed. You will be able to access, open, edit, print, and save the RTF files provided with this book with most word processing programs such as Microsoft *Word*, Windows *WordPad*, and recent versions of *WordPerfect*.

Editing RTFs

Here are some general instructions about editing RTF forms in your word processing program. Refer to the book's instructions and sample agreements for help about what should go in each blank.

- **Underlines.** Underlines indicate where to enter information. After filling in the needed text, delete the underline. In most word processing programs you can do this by highlighting the underlined portion and typing CTRL-U.
- **Bracketed and italicized text.** Bracketed and italicized text indicates instructions. Be sure to remove all instructional text before you finalize your document.
- **Optional text.** Optional text gives you the choice to include or exclude text. Delete any optional text you don't want to use. Renumber numbered items, if necessary.
- **Alternative text.** Alternative text gives you the choice between two or more text options. Delete those options you don't want to use. Renumber numbered items, if necessary.
- **Signature lines.** Signature lines should appear on a page with at least some text from the document itself.

Every word processing program uses different commands to open, format, save, and print documents, so refer to your software's help documents for help using your program. Nolo cannot provide technical support for questions about how to use your computer or your software.

CAUTION

In accordance with U.S. copyright laws, the forms provided by this book are for your personal use only.

List of Forms Available on the Nolo Website

To download any of the files listed on the following pages go to:
www.nolo.com/back-of-book/PART.html

Form Title	File Name
Partnership Agreement	Partnership.rtf
Short-Form Partnership Agreement	ShortForm.rtf

Partnership Agreements

Partnership Agreement

Short-Form Partnership Agreement

Partnership Agreement

[Mandatory. Fill in.]

☐ This Partnership Agreement is entered into and effective as of _____, 20_____,

by: _____

_____, the partners.

1. NAME *[Mandatory. Fill in first clause and second if different partnership business name.]*

☐ The name of the partnership shall be_____

_____.

☐ The name of the partnership business shall be _____

_____.

2. TERM OF THE PARTNERSHIP *[Mandatory. Fill in one of the following.]*

Lasts Until Dissolved on Death of Partner

☐ The partnership shall last until it is dissolved by all the partners, or a partner leaves, for any reason, including death.

Lasts Until Dissolved or Partner Withdraws

☐ The partnership shall last until it is dissolved by all the partners or until a partner withdraws, retires, dies, or otherwise leaves the partnership, under Sections _____ and _____ of this Agreement.

Lasts for Set Term of Years

☐ The partnership shall commence as of the date of this Agreement and shall continue for a period of _____ years, at which time it shall be dissolved and its affairs wound up.

Lasts Until Set Event

☐ The partnership shall continue until _____

_____, at which time it shall be dissolved and its affairs wound up.

3. PURPOSE OF THE PARTNERSHIP [*Mandatory. Fill in.*]

☐ The purpose of the partnership is: _____

_____

_____

_____

_____.

Statement of the Partners' Goals [*Optional. Fill in if desired.*]

☐ The specific purpose of the partnerships are set out above. In addition, the goals and dreams of each partner are set out below. The partners understand that this clause is not legally binding, but include it in the Partnership Agreement as a record of their hopes and intentions:

_____

_____

_____

_____

_____

_____

_____

_____

_____.

4. CONTRIBUTIONS

a. **Contributions of Cash** [*Mandatory. Fill in one or more of the following clauses as applicable.*]

Equal Cash Contribution

☐ The initial capital of the partnership shall be a total of $_____ . Each partner shall contribute an equal share amounting to $_____ , no later than _____ , 20___. Each partner shall own an equal share of the business.

Unequal Cash Contribution

☐ The initial capital of the partnership shall consist of cash to be contributed by the partners in the following amounts:

Name	Amount
_____	$_____
_____	$_____
_____	$_____

Each partner's contribution shall be paid in full by _____, 20_____.

Each partner's ownership share of the business shall be:

Name	Share
_____	_____
_____	_____
_____	_____

Equal Cash Contributions, With a Partner Lending Additional Cash

☐ The initial capital of the partnership shall be a total of $_____. Each partner shall contribute an equal share amounting to $_____, no later than _____, 20_____. In addition, _____ shall lend the partnership $_____ by _____, 20____. The partnership shall pay _____ percent interest on the loan.

Unequal Cash Contributions, to Be Equalized by One Partner's Extra Work in the Business

☐ The initial capital of the partnership shall consist of cash to be contributed by the partners in the following amounts:

Name	Amount
_____	$_____
_____	$_____
_____	$_____

Each partner's contribution shall be paid in full by _____, 20___. In addition, to equalize the contributions, _____ shall contribute an extra _____ hours of work valued at $_____ until the amount contributed by all partners is equal.

Deferred Contributions

Monthly Installments

☐ _____ shall be a partner, but shall

not make any contribution of cash or property to the initial capital of the partnership.

_____ shall subsequently contribute to the partnership

capital, and _____ capital account shall be credited, in the

amount of $_____ per month, beginning _____, 20____, until

_____ has contributed the sum of $_____.

Contribution Out of Profit

☐ _____ shall be a partner, but shall

not make any contribution of cash or property to the initial capital of the partnership.

_____ shall subsequently contribute to the partnership capital,

and _____ capital account shall be credited _____ percent

of _____ share of the partnership profits for each fiscal year, beginning

_____, 20____, until _____ has contributed the amount of $_____.

b. Payment of Interest on Contributed Capital [*Mandatory. Fill in one of the following—
most partnerships choose the first option.*]

No Interest Paid

☐ No partner shall be entitled to receive any interest on any capital contribution.

Interest to Be Paid

☐ _____ shall be entitled to interest on his or her

capital contribution accruing at the rate of _____ percent per year from the date

the contribution is paid. This interest shall be treated as an expense to be charged

against income on the partnership books and shall be paid to the partner entitled to it

_____

_____

_____.

c. Contributions of Property [*Fill in if applicable.*]

Specific Property Contributed

☐ _____

shall contribute property valued at $_____, consisting of _____

_____ by _____, 20____.

Loans of Property to the Partnership

☐ In addition to the capital contributions defined in this Agreement, some partners have or will lend to the partnership additional items of property, as specified below:

_____

shall lend _____

_____.

shall lend _____

_____.

Each item of property lent to the partnership shall remain the separate property of the lending partner and shall be returned to that partner _____.

d. Contributions of Intellectual Property [*Optional. Fill in one of the following if partnership will use intellectual property.*]

Intellectual Property—Ownership Transferred to the Partnership

☐ _____, the owner of

_____, hereby agrees to transfer

all _____ interest in this _____ to the partnership with

the understanding that all _____ interest in the _____,

including the sole right to license derivative works, shall vest in, and be owned by, the

partnership and shall not be _____ separate property. In exchange for this transfer, it is

agreed that _____ shall be credited

with a contribution of $_____ to the partnership. No sale or assignment of,

or grant of license under, the _____ shall be made

without the consent of all the partners. Any monies resulting from any such sale,

assignment, or grant of license shall be divided _____.

Intellectual Property—Only Use Transferred to the Partnership

☐ _____, the owner of

_____,

hereby contributes to the partnership the nonexclusive use of that _____,

with the understanding that _____ shall retain sole ownership of the

_____, along with the sole right to license its use to third parties,

and it shall not become a partnership asset. _____

further agrees that until the termination of the partnership, or until _____

death or retirement from it, _____ will not, without the consent of all

other partners, sell, assign, or grant licenses under this _____.

Any money accruing from a sale or assignment of, or the grant of license under, such

_____, which are so authorized, shall be the sole

property of _____. For the purpose

of profit-sharing only, and not for participation in the distribution upon the termination

and winding up of the partnership, the partnership will credit _____

_____ with a contribution in the amount of $_____.

e. **Contributions of Service** [*Fill in one or both of the following if applicable.*]

Contribution of Services

☐ _____.

shall make no cash or property contribution at the commencement of the partnership.

_____ shall donate _____ and

energies to the partnership for a period of _____ and for those services

_____ shall be entitled to _____ percent ownership of the business.

Contribution of Profits From Service Partner

☐ Should _____ share of the profits, as

defined in this Agreement, exceed _____, _____

shall contribute the excess to _____ capital account in the business until the

total amount of _____ capital account shall _____.

---

f. Failure to Make Initial Contribution [*Mandatory. Fill in one or more of the following.*]

Partnership Dissolves

☐ If any partner fails to pay his or her initial contribution to the partnership as required by this Agreement, the partnership shall immediately dissolve and each partner who has paid all or any portion of his or her initial contribution to the partnership's capital shall be entitled to a return of the funds and properties he or she contributed.

Partnership Continues for Partners Who Have Made Contributions, and No Additional Contribution Required

☐ If any partner fails to pay his or her contribution to the partnership's capital as required by this Agreement, the partnership shall not dissolve or terminate, but it shall continue as a partnership of only the partners who have made their initial capital contributions as required and without any partner who has failed to do so. In that case, the share in the partnership's profits and losses allocated under this Agreement to any partner who has failed to make his or her initial contribution shall be reallocated to the remaining partners in proportion to their respective shares of partnership profits and losses as specified in this Agreement.

Partnership Continues—Additional Contributions Are Required

☐ If any partner fails to pay his or her initial contributions to the partnership's capital as required by this Agreement, the partnership shall not dissolve or terminate, but shall continue as a partnership of the partners who have made their initial capital contributions and without any partner who shall have failed to do so, but only if the remaining partners pay the initial capital contribution that was to have been made by the noncontributing partner or partners. The partnership shall promptly give written notice of this failure to all partners who have made their initial capital contributions. The notice shall specify the amount not paid. Within _____ days after the notice is given, the remaining partners shall pay the amount of the defaulted contribution in proportion to the respective amount they are required to pay to the partnership's capital under this

Agreement. That share of the profits of the partnership belonging to noncontributing partners shall then be reallocated to the remaining partners in proportion to their respective shares of partnership profits and losses under this Agreement.

Failure of Service Partner to Actually Perform Service

☐ If _____

fails to contribute the services promised, the partnership shall proceed as follows:

_____

_____

_____.

g. Additional Future Contributions [*Optional. Fill in one or more of the following clauses if desired.*]

If Future Contributions Needed

☐ If, at any future time, more money is required to carry on the partnership business, and all partners vote to increase the capital contributions required by partners, the additional capital shall be paid in by the partners _____

_____.

Requirement of Annual Contributions by Partners

☐ Each partner shall contribute annually [_____ *percent of his or her share of each year's profits*] [*or* $_____] to the partnership's capital for a period of _____ years. If any partner fails to make such contribution, _____.

No Voluntary Contributions Without Consent

☐ No partner may make any voluntary contribution to the partnership without the written consent of all the other partners.

5. PROFITS AND LOSSES

a. Distribution of Profits and Losses [*Mandatory. Fill in one of the following.*]

Equal Shares

☐ The partners will share all profits equally, and they will be distributed _____

_____

_____. All losses of the partnership shall also be shared equally.

Unequal Shares: Set Percentages

☐ The partnership profits and losses shall be shared among the partners as follows:

Name	Percentage
_____	_____ %
_____	_____ %
_____	_____ %
_____	_____ %

Unequal Shares: Different Percentages for Profits and Losses

☐ The partnership profits and losses shall be shared among the partners as follows:

Name	Percentage of Profits	Percentage of Losses
_____	_____ %	_____ %
_____	_____ %	_____ %
_____	_____ %	_____ %
_____	_____ %	_____ %

Unequal Shares: Profits and Losses Keyed to Capital Contributions

☐ The partnership's profits and losses shall be shared by the partners in the same proportions as their initial contributions of capital bear to each other.

b. **Draws to Partners** [*Mandatory. Fill in one of the following.*]

Draws Authorized

☐ Partners _____ and

_____ are entitled to draws from

expected partnership profits. The amount of each draw will be determined by a vote of

the partners. The draws shall be paid _____

_____.

Draws Prohibited

☐ No partner shall be entitled to any draw against partnership profits. Distributions shall

be made only as provided in this Agreement, or upon subsequent unanimous written

agreement of the partners.

c. **Draws Exceeding Partners' Actual Shares of Profits to Become Loans to Partners**
[*Optional. Fill in if desired.*]

☐ Notwithstanding the provisions of this Agreement governing drawing permitted by

partners, to the extent any partner's withdrawals for draws under those provisions

during any fiscal year of the partnership exceed his or her share in the partnership's

profits, the excess shall be regarded as a loan from the partnership to him or her that

he or she is obligated to repay within _____ days after the end of that fiscal year.

d. **Retention of Profits for Business Needs** [*Optional. Fill in one or both clauses if desired.*]

General Limitation on Distribution to Retain Cash for Business Needs

☐ In determining the amount of profits available for distribution, allowance will be made

for the fact that some money must remain undistributed and available as working

capital as determined by _____.

Specific Limitation on Distribution to Retain Cash for Business Needs

☐ The aggregate amounts distributed to the partners from the partnership profits shall

not exceed _____ percent of any net income above $_____.

6. MANAGEMENT POWERS AND DUTIES

a. Work Contribution [*Optional. Fill in or use one or more clauses as desired.*]

Skills Contributed

☐ Each partner named below shall participate in the business by working in the manner described:

Partner   Type of Work

_____   _____

_____   _____

_____   _____

_____   _____

Hours Worked

☐ Except for vacations, holidays, and times of illness, each partner shall work _____ hours per week on partnership business.

Leaves of Absence

☐ Any partner can take a leave of absence from the partnership under the following terms and conditions:

_____

_____

_____

_____.

All Partners Work in Business

☐ All partners shall be actively involved and materially participate in the management and operation of the partnership business.

b. Decisions [*Mandatory. Fill in one of the following.*]

All Decisions Unanimous

☐ All partnership decisions must be made by the unanimous agreement of all partners.

Major/Minor Decisions

☐ All major decisions of the partnership business must be made by a unanimous decision of all partners. Minor business decisions may be made by an individual partner. Major decisions are defined as: _____

_____

_____ .

c. Unequal Management Powers [*Optional. Fill in one if desired.*]

In Accordance With Contributed Capital

☐ Each partner shall participate in the management of the business. In exercising the powers of management, each partner's vote shall be in proportion to his or her interest in the partnership's capital.

By Fixed Percentage as Agreed on by Partners

☐ In the management, control, and direction of the business, the partners shall have the following percentages of voting power:

Name	Percentage
_____	_____ %
_____	_____ %
_____	_____ %
_____	_____ %

d. Financial Matters [*Optional. Fill in or use one or more as desired.*]

Periodic Accountings

☐ Accountings of _____ shall be made every _____ .

Accounting on Request by a Partner

☐ Accountings of any aspect of partnership business shall be made upon written request by any partner.

Accountant to Determine Profits and Losses

☐ The partnership's net profit or net loss for each fiscal year shall be determined as soon as practicable after the close of that fiscal year. This should be done by a certified public accountant, _____ , in accordance with the accounting principles employed in the preparation of the federal income tax return filed by the partnership for that year, but without a special provision for tax-exempt or partially tax-exempt income.

Power to Borrow Money

☐ A partner can borrow money on behalf of the partnership in excess of $_____ only with prior consent of all partners.

Expense Accounts Authorized

☐ An expense account, not to exceed $_____ per month, shall be set up for each partner for his or her actual, reasonable, and necessary expenses during the course of the business. Each partner shall keep an itemized record of these expenses and be paid once monthly for them on submission of the record.

Expense Accounts Not Authorized

☐ The partners individually and personally shall assume and pay:

- All expenses for the entertainment of persons having business relations with the partnership.
- Expenses associated with usual business activities.

Signature Required on Partnership Checks

☐ All partnership funds shall be deposited in the name of the partnership and shall be subject to withdrawal only on the signatures of at least _____ partners.

Prohibition Against Commingling

☐ All partnership funds shall be deposited only in bank accounts bearing the partnership name.

For Businesses Receiving Funds to Be Held in a Trust Account

☐ All trust and other similar funds shall be deposited in a trust account established in the partnership's name at _____ bank, and shall be kept separate and not mingled with any other funds of the partnership.

Meetings

☐ For the purpose of discussing matters of general interest to the partnership, together with the conduct of its business, partners shall meet _____ _____ or at such other times agreed upon by the majority of the partners.

Maintenance of Records

☐ Proper and complete books of account of the partnership business shall be kept at the partnership's principal place of business and shall be open to inspection by any of the partners or their accredited representative at any reasonable time during business hours.

Vacation

☐ Each partner shall be entitled to _____ weeks paid [*or* unpaid] vacation per year.

Sick Leave

☐ The partnership's sick leave policy for partners is:

_____

_____

_____.

e. Outside Business Activities [*Mandatory. Fill in one of the following.*]

Permitted, Except for Direct Competition

☐ Any partner may be engaged in one or more other businesses as well as the business of the partnership, but only to the extent that this activity does not directly and materially interfere with the business of the partnership and does not conflict with the time commitments and other obligations of that partner to the partnership under this Agreement. Neither the partnership nor any other partner shall have any right to any income or profit derived by a partner from any business activity permitted under this section.

Permitted

☐ It is understood and agreed that each partner may engage in other businesses, including enterprises in competition with the partnership. The partners need not offer any business opportunities to the partnership, but may take advantage of those opportunities for their own accounts or for the accounts of other partnerships or enterprises with which they are associated. Neither the partnership nor any other partner shall have any right to any income or profit derived by a partner from any enterprise or opportunity permitted by this section.

Specific Activities Permitted

☐ The list below specifies business activities that each partner plans or may do outside of the partnership business. Each partner is expressly authorized to engage in these activities if he or she so desires:

_____

_____

_____

_____

_____

_____

_____ .

Restricted

☐ As long as any partner is a member of the partnership, he or she shall devote his or her full work time and energies to the conduct of partnership business, and shall not be actively engaged in the conduct of any other business for compensation or a share in profits as an employee, officer, agent, proprietor, partner, or stockholder. This prohibition shall not prevent him or her from being a passive investor in any enterprise, however, if he or she is not actively engaged in its business and does not exercise control over it. Neither the partnership nor any other partner shall have any right to any income or profit derived from any such passive investment.

f. Ownership of Business Assets [*Optional. Fill in as needed.*]

Trade Secrets

☐ All trade secrets used or developed by the partnership, including customer lists and sources of supplies, will be owned and controlled by the partnership.

Patents

☐ Any ideas developed by one or more partners pertaining to partnership business that are the subject of an application for a patent shall be partnership property.

Copyrights

☐ All copyrighted materials in the partnership name are, and shall remain, partnership property.

Business Name

☐ The partnership business name of _____
_____ shall be partnership property. In the event of the departure of a partner and/or dissolution of the partnership, control and ownership of the partnership business name shall be determined pursuant to this Agreement.

g. Provision for a Managing Partner [*Optional. Fill in as needed.*]

Authority of Managing Partner

☐ The managing partner shall be _____.

The managing partner shall have control over the business of the partnership and assume direction of its business operations. The managing partner shall consult and confer as far as practicable with the nonmanaging partners, but the power of decision shall be vested in the managing partner. The managing partner's power and duties shall include control over the partnership's books and records and hiring any independent certified public accountant the managing partner deems necessary for this purpose. On the managing partner's death, resignation, or other disability, a new managing partner shall be selected by a majority of the partners.

Limited Authority for Managing Partner

☐ The managing partner shall be _____.

The managing partner shall have control over routine business transactions and day-to-day operating decisions. The managing partner shall not make any major or basic decisions without consent of a majority of the partners. A major or basic decision is defined as: _____

_____

_____

Salary of Managing Partner

☐ The managing partner shall be paid a monthly salary of $_____ or such other amount that may be determined by the unanimous written agreement of the partners. This salary shall be treated as a partnership expense in determining its profits or losses.

Managing Partner Handles All Money of the Partnership

☐ All partnership funds shall be deposited in the partnership's name and shall be subject to withdrawal only on the signature of the managing partner.

Managing Partner Handles Operating Fund Only

☐   All partnership funds shall be deposited in the partnership's name and shall be subject to withdrawal only on the signatures of at least _____ partners, except that a separate account may be maintained with a balance never to exceed $_____. The amounts in that separate account shall be subject to withdrawal on the signature of the managing partner.

7. AMENDMENTS AND NEW PARTNERS

a. Amendments [*Mandatory. Fill in one of the following.*]

By Unanimous Agreement

☐   This Agreement may be amended only by written consent of all partners.

As Specified

☐   This Agreement may be amended by _____

_____.

b. Admission of New Partner(s) [*Mandatory. Fill in one of the following.*]

Addition by Unanimous Written Agreement of All Partners

☐   A new partner or partners may be added to the partnership only by unanimous written consent of all existing partners.

Addition by Less Than All Partners

☐   A new partner may be admitted to the partnership with the written approval of

_____.

c. Admitting a New Partner When You've Failed to Plan Ahead [*Optional. Fill in if needed.*]

☐   _____

_____ have been engaged in business at

_____

as a partnership under the firm name of _____

_____. They now intend to

admit _____ to their partnership, and all

the members of the expanded partnership desire to amend and clarify the terms and

conditions of their Partnership Agreement and to reduce their agreement to writing.

d. No Dissolution of the Partnership When a New Partner Joins [*Mandatory—unless dissolution is desired when new partner joins.*]

☐ Admission of a new partner shall not cause dissolution of the underlying partnership business, which will be continued by the new partnership entity.

e. The Incoming Partner's Liability for Existing Partnership Debts [*Optional. Usually used only when a new partner actually joins partnership.*]

Not Responsible for Partnership Debts Before Becoming Partners

☐ _____ shall not be

personally responsible for, or assume any liability for, any debts of _____

_____ incurred on or before _____, 20_____.

Responsible for Partnership Debts From Set Date

☐ _____ hereby

expressly assumes personal liability for debts of _____

_____ incurred on or before _____, 20_____,

equal to the amount of his or her contribution to the partnership, totaling $_____.

Responsible for All Partnership Debts

☐ _____

hereby expressly assumes full personal liability equal to the personal liability of all other

partners in the partnership of _____

_____ for all partnership debts and obligations whenever incurred.

8. TRANSFER OF A PARTNER'S INTEREST

a. **Sale** [*Mandatory. Use one of the following clauses.*]

Sale to Partnership or Partners at Their Option

☐ If any partner leaves the partnership, for whatever reason, whether he or she quits, withdraws, is expelled, retires, becomes mentally or physically incapacitated or unable to function as a partner, or dies, or if the partner attempts to or is ordered to transfer his or her interest, whether voluntarily or involuntarily, he or she, or his or her estate, shall be obligated to sell his or her interest in the partnership to the remaining partner or partners, who have the option, but not the obligation, to buy that interest. However, if the departing partner receives a bona fide offer from a prospective outside buyer, the Right of First Refusal Clause of this Agreement shall apply.

Sale to Partner at His or Her Option [*for a two-person partnership*]

☐ If either partner leaves the partnership, for whatever reason, whether he or she quits, withdraws, retires, becomes mentally or physically incapacitated or unable to function as a partner, or dies, or if the partner attempts to or is ordered to transfer his or her interest, whether voluntarily or involuntarily, he or she, or his or her estate, shall be obligated to sell his or her interest in the partnership to the remaining owner, who has the option, but not the obligation, to buy that interest. However, if the departing partner receives a bona fide offer from a prospective outside buyer, the Right of First Refusal Clause of this Agreement shall apply.

b. **The Right of First Refusal Upon Offer From Outside** [*Mandatory.*]

☐ If any partner receives a bona fide, legitimate offer, whether or not solicited by him or her, from a person not a partner, to purchase all of his or her interest in the partnership, and if the partner receiving the offer is willing to accept it, he or she shall give written notice of the amount and terms of the offer, the identity of the proposed buyer, and his or her willingness to accept the offer to each of the other partners. The other partner or partners shall have the option, within _____ days after the notice is given, to purchase that partner's interest on the same terms as those contained in the offer.

c. Refusal of the Remaining Partners to Buy [*Mandatory.*]

☐ If the remaining partner or partners do not purchase the departing partner's share of the business, under the terms provided in this Agreement, within _____ _____ the entire business of the partnership shall be put up for sale, and listed with the appropriate sales agencies, agents, or brokers.

d. Requiring Advance Notice of Withdrawal [*Generally mandatory.*]

☐ Unless physically prevented from giving notice, a partner shall give _____ _____ written advance notice of his or her intention to leave the partnership. If he or she fails to do so, _____.

e. Conflicts Regarding Right to Buy [*Mandatory. Fill in one of the following.*]

The Coin Flip

☐ If the partners cannot agree on who has the right to purchase the other partners' interest in the business, that right shall be determined by the flip of a coin [*optional* to be flipped by _____].

Auction Bidding

☐ If the partners cannot agree who has the right to purchase the other partners' interest in the business, that right shall be determined by an auction, where each group of partners shall bid on the business. The group eventually offering the highest bid shall have the right to buy the lower bidders' shares of the business. The buying group shall pay for the purchased share of the business under the terms provided in this Agreement.

9. BUY-SELL AGREEMENT

a. Determining the Value of the Business [*Mandatory. Fill in one of the following.*]

Asset Valuation Method

☐ Except as otherwise provided in this Agreement, the value of the partnership shall be made by determining the net worth of the partnership as of the date a partner leaves, for any reason. Net worth is defined as the market value, as of that date, of the following assets:

1. All tangible property, real or personal, owned by the business;

2. All the liquid assets owned by the business, including cash on hand, bank deposits and CDs, or other monies;

3. All accounts receivable;

4. All earned but unbilled fees;

5. All money presently earned for work in progress;

6. Less the total amount of all debts owed by the business.

Set-Dollar Method

☐ Except as otherwise provided in this Agreement, the value of a partner's interest in the partnership shall be determined as follows:

1. Within _____ days after the end of each fiscal year of the partnership, the partners shall determine the partnership's value by unanimous written agreement, and that value shall remain in effect from the date of that written determination until the next such written determination.

2. Should the partners be unable to agree on a value or otherwise fail to make any such determination, the partnership's value shall be the greater of (a) the value last established under this section, or (b)

_____

_____

_____

_____

_____

_____

_____ .

3. _____

_____

_____

_____

_____

_____

_____ .

Postdeparture Appraisal

☐ Except as otherwise provided in this Agreement, the value of the partnership shall be determined by an independent appraisal conducted, if possible, by _____

_____. If all partners cannot agree on an appraiser, the departing partner and the remaining partners shall each select an independent appraiser. If the two selected appraisers are unable to agree on the fair market value of the partnership business, then the two appraisers shall mutually select a third appraiser to determine the fair market value.

The appraisal shall be commenced within _____ days of the partner's departure from the partnership. The partnership and the departing partner shall share the cost of the appraisal equally.

The Capitalization-of-Earnings Method

☐ Except as otherwise provided in this Agreement, the value of the partnership shall be determined as follows:

1. The average yearly earnings of the business shall be calculated for the preceding

   _____.

2. "Earnings," as used in this clause, is defined as: _____.

3. The average yearly earnings shall then be multiplied by a multiple of _____ to give the value of the business, except as provided for in Section 4, below;

4. Additional factors: _____

   _____

   _____.

b. Varying the Buyout Price [*Optional. Use if desired.*]

☐ The preceding method for calculating the value of the business shall be varied as stated below, for the reasons stated below: _____

_____

_____

_____

_____.

c. **Valuation Revision** [*Optional. Use one or both of the following if desired.*]

Revision of Valuation Method

☐ The partners agree that _____ years after the commencement of the business, they will revise this valuation clause so that the method used will best reflect the worth of the business.

Revision of Valuation Method to Include Goodwill

☐ The partners understand and agree that the preceding business valuation clause may not fully and adequately reflect the worth of the business after it has been successfully established, if the business has earned goodwill or has other valuable intangible assets. Therefore, the partners agree that _____ after the commencement of the business they will meet to consider amending this business valuation clause to include a method that will reflect any goodwill earned by the business.

d. **Insurance Proceeds: Disability or Death of a Partner** [*Optional. Use if desired.*]

☐ If a partner becomes disabled or dies, the value of his or her interest in the partnership, including for estate purposes, shall be the proceeds paid by the disability or death insurance policy maintained by the partnership [*or* other partners] for that partner.

e. **Consent of Spouse** [*Optional. Use if desired.*]

☐ I, _____, the _____ of _____, have read and understand this Partnership Agreement and hereby consent to all clauses and terms in it. I specifically agree that the business valuation method contained in the Agreement shall be used in any legal proceeding to determine the value of any interest I may have in the business.

Dated: _____ Signature: _____

f. Payments [*Mandatory. Fill in one of the following.*]

Equal Monthly Payments

☐ Whenever the partnership is obligated or chooses to purchase a partner's interest in the partnership, it shall pay for that interest by promissory note of the partnership. Any promissory note shall be dated as of the effective date of the purchase, shall mature in not more than _____ years, shall be payable in equal installments that come due monthly [and shall bear interest at the rate of _____ percent per annum] [and may, at the partnership's option, be subordinated to existing and future debts to banks and other institutional lenders for money borrowed]. The first payment shall be made _____ days after the date of the promissory note.

Lump Sum, Then Equal Monthly Payments

☐ Whenever the partnership is obligated to, or chooses to, purchase a partner's interest in the partnership, it shall pay for that interest as follows:

First: It shall pay the departing partner _____ within _____.

Second: After that initial payment, it shall pay the balance owed by promissory note of the partnership. Any promissory note shall be dated as of the effective date of the purchase, shall mature in not more than _____ years, shall be payable in equal installments that come due monthly [and shall bear interest at the rate of _____ percent per annum] [and may, at the partnership's option, be subordinated to existing and future debts to banks and other institutional lenders for money borrowed]. The first payment shall be made _____ days after the date of the promissory note.

Cash Payment

☐ Whenever the partnership is obligated or chooses to purchase a partner's interest in the partnership, it shall pay for that interest in cash within _____.

g. Assumption of Departing Partner's Liabilities [*Optional. Use if desired.*]

☐ The continuing partnership shall pay, as they come due, all partnership debts and obligations that exist on the date a partner leaves the partnership, and shall hold the departing partner harmless from any claim arising from these debts and obligations.

10. CONTINUITY OF PARTNERSHIP BUSINESS

a. Partnership Continues [*Generally mandatory and desired by partnership.*]

☐ In the case of a partner's death, permanent disability, retirement, voluntary withdrawal, expulsion from the partnership, or death, the partnership shall not dissolve or terminate, but its business shall continue without interruption and without any break in continuity. On the disability, retirement, withdrawal, expulsion, or death of any partner, the others shall not liquidate or wind up the affairs of the partnership, but shall continue to conduct a partnership under the terms of this Agreement.

b. Noncompetition Clause [*Optional. Use if desired.*]

☐ On the voluntary withdrawal, permanent disability, retirement, death, or expulsion of any partner, that partner shall not carry on a business the same as or similar to the business of the partnership within the _____ for a period of _____.

c. Control of the Business Name [*Mandatory. Fill in one of the following.*]

Partnership Continues to Own Name

☐ The partnership business name of _____ is owned by the partnership. Should any partner cease to be a member of the partnership, the partnership shall continue to retain exclusive ownership and right to use the partnership business name.

One Partner Owns Name

☐ The partnership business name of _____
shall be solely owned by _____,
if _____ ceases to be a partner.

Control of Name to Be Decided at Later Date

☐ The partnership business name of _____
is owned by the partnership. Should any person cease to be a partner and desire to use the partnership business name, and the remaining partners desire to continue the

---

partnership and continue use of the partnership business name, ownership and control of the partnership business name shall be decided by _____ _____.

Dissolution: Majority Owns Name

☐ In the event of dissolution, the partnership business name of _____ _____ _____ shall be owned by a majority of the former partners. Any other former partner is not entitled to ownership or use of the partnership business name.

d. Expulsion of a Partner [*Optional. Use if desired.*]

☐ A partner may be expelled from the partnership by a vote of _____ _____ _____ _____ _____.

Expulsion shall become effective when written notice of expulsion is served on the expelled partner. When the expulsion becomes effective, the expelled partner's right to participate in the partnership's profits and his or her other rights, powers, and authority as a partner of the partnership shall terminate. An expelled partner shall be entitled to receive the value of his or her interest in the partnership, as that value is defined in this Agreement.

e. A Partner's Bankruptcy and Expulsion [*Optional. Commonly used.*]

☐ Notwithstanding any other provision of this Agreement, a partner shall cease to be a partner and shall have no interest in common with the remaining partners or in partnership property when the partner does any of the following:

1. Obtains or becomes subject to an order of relief under the Bankruptcy Code.
2. Obtains or becomes subject to an order or decree of insolvency under state law.
3. Makes an assignment for the benefit of creditors.

4. Consents to or accepts the appointment of a receiver or trustee to any substantial part of his or her assets that is not vacated within _____ days.

5. Consents to or accepts an attachment or execution of any substantial part of his or her assets that is not released within _____ days.

From the date of any of the preceding events, he or she shall be considered as a seller to the partnership of his or her interest in the partnership as set forth in this Agreement.

If a partner is expelled for one of the above reasons, the partnership shall not be dissolved, but shall continue to function without interruption.

f. Expulsion and Arbitration [*Optional. Commonly used.*]

☐ Any decision of expulsion made by the partners pursuant to this Agreement shall be final and shall not be subject to arbitration or other review, including review by any court.

g. Insurance and Partner's Estate Planning [*Optional. Use one or more of the following if desired.*]

Cross-Purchase of Life Insurance

☐ Each partner shall purchase and maintain life insurance [and disability insurance] on the life of each other partner in the face value of $_____.

Partnership Insurance Policies

☐ The life insurance policies owned by the partnership on the lives of each partner are assets of the partnership only insofar as they have cash surrender value preceding the death of a partner.

Insurance Polices and Partner's Departure

☐ On the withdrawal or termination of any partner for any reason other than his or her death [*add* "or disability" *if the partners purchase disability insurance on each other*], any insurance policies on his or her life ["or health"], for which the partnership paid the premiums, shall be delivered to that partner and become his or her separate property. If the policy has a cash surrender value, that amount shall be paid to the partnership by the withdrawing partner, or offset against the partnership's obligations to him or her.

---

11. MEDIATION AND ARBITRATION [*Mandatory. Fill in one or more of the following.*]

Mediation

☐ 1. The partners agree that, except as otherwise provided in this Agreement, any dispute arising out of this Agreement or the partnership business shall first be resolved by mediation, if possible. The partners are aware that mediation is a voluntary process, and pledge to cooperate fully and fairly with the mediator in any attempt to reach a mutually satisfactory compromise to a dispute.

2. The mediator shall be _____.

3. If any partner to a dispute feels it cannot be resolved by the partners themselves, after mediation has been attempted, he or she shall so notify the other partners, and the mediator, in writing.

4. Mediation shall commence within ____ days of this notice of request for mediation.

5. Any decision reached by mediation shall be reduced to writing, signed by all partners, and be binding on them.

6. The costs of mediation shall be shared equally by all partners to the dispute.

Combining Mediation With Arbitration [*Optional Clause to include with Mediation.*]

☐ If the partners cannot resolve the dispute by mediation, the dispute shall be arbitrated as provided in the arbitration clause of this Agreement.

Time for Mediation [*Optional Clause to include with Mediation.*]

☐ If the partners have not resolved their dispute within _____ of the commencement of mediation, the partners shall have failed to have resolved their dispute by mediation under this Agreement, and the dispute shall be arbitrated.

Arbitration

Arbitration With One Arbitrator

☐ 1. The partners agree that, except as otherwise provided in this Agreement, any dispute arising out of this Agreement, or the partnership business, shall be arbitrated under the terms of this clause. The arbitration shall be carried out by a single arbitrator _____

_____

_____.

Any arbitration shall be held as follows: _____

_____.

2. The partner(s) initiating the arbitration procedure shall inform the other partner(s) in writing of the nature of the dispute at the same time that he or she notifies the arbitrator.

3. Within _____ days from receipt of this notice, the other partners shall reply in writing, stating their views of the nature of the dispute.

4. The arbitrator shall hold a hearing on the dispute within seven (7) days after the reply of the other partner(s). Each partner shall be entitled to present whatever oral or written statements he or she wishes and may present witnesses. No partner may be represented by a lawyer or any third party.

5. The arbitrator shall make his or her decision in writing.

6. If the partner(s) to whom the demand for arbitration is directed fails to respond within the proper time limit, the partner(s) initiating the arbitration must give the other an additional five (5) days' written notice of "intention to proceed to arbitration." If there is still no response, the partner(s) initiating the arbitration may proceed with the arbitration before the arbitrator, and his or her award shall be binding.

7. The cost of arbitration shall be borne by the partners as the arbitrator shall direct.

8. The arbitration award shall be conclusive and binding on the partners and shall be set forth in such a way that a formal judgment can be entered in the court having jurisdiction over the dispute if either party so desires.

Arbitration With Three Arbitrators

☐ The partners agree that, except as otherwise provided in this Agreement, any dispute arising out of this Agreement or the partnership business shall be arbitrated under the terms of this clause. The arbitration shall be carried out by three arbitrators. Each partner or side to the dispute shall appoint one arbitrator. The two designated arbitrators shall appoint the third arbitrator.

The arbitration shall be carried out as follows:

1. The partner(s) initiating the arbitration procedure shall inform the other partner(s) in writing of the nature of the dispute at the same time that they designate one arbitrator.

2. Within ____ days from receipt of this notice, the other partners shall reply in writing naming the second arbitrator, and stating their view of the nature of the dispute.

3. The two designated arbitrators shall name a third arbitrator within ten (10) days from the date the second arbitrator is named. If they cannot agree _____

   _____

   _____ .

4. An arbitration meeting shall be held within _____ days after the third arbitrator is named.

5. Each partner shall be entitled to present whatever oral or written statements he or she wishes and may present witnesses. No partner may be represented by a lawyer or any third party.

6. The arbitrators shall make their decision in writing.

7. If the partner(s) to whom the demand for arbitration is directed fails to respond within the proper time limit, the partner(s) initiating the arbitration must give the other an additional five (5) days' written notice of "intention to proceed to arbitration." If there is still no response, the partner(s) initiating the arbitration may proceed with the arbitration before the arbitrators, and their award shall be binding.

8. The cost of arbitration shall be borne by the partners as the arbitrators shall direct.

9. The arbitration award shall be conclusive and binding on the partners and shall be set forth in such a way that a formal judgment can be entered in the court having jurisdiction over the dispute if either party so desires.

12. GENERAL PROVISIONS [*Mandatory. Fill in all of the following clauses.*]

State Law

☐ The partners have formed this general partnership under the laws of the State of _____, intending to be legally bound thereby.

Attached Papers Incorporated

☐ Any attached sheet or document shall be regarded as fully contained in this Partnership Agreement.

Agreement Is All-Inclusive

☐ This Agreement contains the entire understanding of the partners regarding their rights and duties in the partnership. Any alleged oral representations of modifications concerning this Agreement shall be of no force or effect unless contained in a subsequent written modification signed by all partners.

Binding on All Successors and Inheritors

☐ This Agreement shall be binding on and for the benefit of the respective successors, inheritors, assigns, and personal representatives of the partners, except to the extent of any contrary provision in the Agreement.

Severability

☐ If any term, provision, or condition of this Agreement is held by a court of competent jurisdiction to be invalid, void, or unenforceable, the rest of the Agreement shall remain in full force and effect and shall in no way be affected, impaired, or invalidated.

13. ADDITIONAL PROVISIONS [*Optional.*]

_____

_____

_____

_____

_____

_____.

Signature: _____ Dated: _____

Signature: _____ Dated: _____

Signature: _____ Dated: _____

Short-Form Partnership Agreement

_____ , _____ ,

_____ , _____ , and

_____ , agree as follows:

1. That as of _____ , 20_____ , they are partners in a

   business known as _____

   _____

   _____

   _____ .

2. That the general purpose of the business is _____

   _____

   _____

   _____ .

3. That the partners now agree that _____

   _____

   _____

   _____ .

4. That the partners further agree that they will prepare, by _____ , 20_____ ,

   a final and complete partnership agreement governing the partnership, and that the

   agreement will cover at least:

   - contributions of each partner to the partnership
   - distribution of profits and losses
   - management powers and responsibilities
   - admission of new partners
   - the departure of a partner for any reason, and
   - arbitration.

To formalize this short-form partnership agreement, each partner has signed his or her name on the date below:

Signature: _____ Dated: _____

Signature: _____ Dated: _____

Signature: _____ Dated: _____

Signature: _____ Dated: _____

Signature: _____ Dated: _____

Signature: _____ Dated: _____

Index

 **NOLO**   *More from Nolo*

Nolo.com offers a large library of legal solutions and forms, created by Nolo's in-house legal editors. These reliable documents can be prepared in minutes.

Create a Document Online

Incorporation. Incorporate your business in any state.

LLC Formation. Gain asset protection and pass-through tax status in any state.

Will. Nolo has helped people make over 2 million wills. Is it time to make or revise yours?

Living Trust (avoid probate). Plan now to save your family the cost, delays, and hassle of probate.

Provisional Patent. Preserve your right to obtain a patent by claiming "patent pending" status.

Download Useful Legal Forms

Nolo.com has hundreds of top quality legal forms available for download:

- bill of sale
- promissory note
- nondisclosure agreement
- LLC operating agreement
- corporate minutes
- commercial lease and sublease
- motor vehicle bill of sale
- consignment agreement
- and many more.

www.nolo.com

On Nolo.com you'll also find:

Books & Software

Nolo publishes hundreds of great books and software programs for consumers and business owners. Order a copy, or download an ebook version instantly, at Nolo.com.

Online Forms

You can quickly and easily make a will or living trust, form an LLC or corporation, apply for a provisional patent, or make hundreds of other forms—online.

Free Legal Information

Thousands of articles answer common questions about everyday legal issues, including wills, bankruptcy, small business formation, divorce, patents, employment, and much more.

Plain-English Legal Dictionary

Stumped by jargon? Look it up in America's most up-to-date source for definitions of legal terms, free at Nolo.com.

Lawyer Directory

Nolo's consumer-friendly lawyer directory provides in-depth profiles of lawyers all over America. You'll find information you need to choose the right lawyer.

PART11